The Wolf Talk

by Shaun Ellis

Rainbow Publishing, England

Illustrations and paintings reproduced with kind permission of Brenda McKetty, Jonathan Truss and Arthur Budge

Photographs reproduced with kind permission of Andy George, Mitsy Jane Tuvey, Chris Porter, A. Braithwaite and David Doughty Cover photograph: Mitsy Jane Tuvey

This first edition first published in 2003 by Rainbow Publishing

PO Box 1044, Haxey, Doncaster. DN9 2JN

A record for this book is available in the British Library

ISBN 1-899057-03-X

Editor Angela White, Doncaster, England.

Printed by PrintingZone, Doncaster. Telephone: 01302 761077

Dedication and Acknowlegements

I would like to dedicate this account of my life with these animals to the many people that have made it all possible. From my time as a small child under the guidance of the many people that matter the most in my life, to those that help shape it, not just with animals, but also with the day to day challenges that life has a nasty habit of throwing at you.

Without the start you all gave me I can truly say that I would not have got this far. I never have, or ever will, forget you.

To the many people that give up their free time to volunteer to help us in the daily running of Wolf Pack Management, without your tireless efforts, often with very little reward and in all weathers, the amount of work that we need to achieve would have almost certainly suffered greatly without your help. Therefore, on behalf of both Jan and myself, a massive thank you.

Now, to the many Native American people, from many differing cultures, who I have worked with over the years. Thank you all for my daily inspiration and the courage that you have inspired in me, as well as the many others that know you.

To all the staff at Wolf Pack Management that make my work with the wolves possible, your constant support is always appreciated, although that appreciation is not always shown because of our busy schedule.

A special thank you must go to my family who have had to make their own personal sacrifices during the many years I have lived away from them. Having to deal with the never-ending lack of financial comfort that they have never once complained about. You are all mature far beyond your years, something I often forget. Let me now take this opportunity to tell you how proud I have become of you all.

A huge thank you must also go out to the entire staff of the safari and wildlife parks, without your support and help none of our research would have been possible.

To my many proof readers and people who helped with the text of this book, not forgetting the very special people who have supplied the many beautiful pictures throughout.

With special thanks to:

Mitsy Tuvey - photographer and proof reader

Jules Tuvey - computer

Angela and Kevin Sampson - keepers

Kate Barron - volunteer keeper

Liz Hammer - keeper

Chris Porter - keeper

Andy George - staff

Scott Williams - work experience

Kayleigh Williams - child minder

Kyra, Beth and Jack

Wellingborough Dog Club

Finally I would like to make a personal dedication to my partner Jan. Her endless support and constant encouragement not only helps me through each and every day but, also brings me through the many ups and downs that we have both encountered whilst working with these animals. Always content to stand in my shadow, she remains every inch a hero of mine as I ever have been of hers. Her strength and dedication to the animals she cares for are a tribute to her hard work. Thank you for your strength, I would have never made it without you.

Shaun

THE WOLF TALK

Contents

Prologue

Try to imagine…

You are standing in an area of open land and you are not alone. Ahead of you, maybe 300 or 350 metres away, is dense forest and concealed at the forest edge is a wolf.

You cannot see him.

You cannot hear him.

You cannot smell him.

The wolf, however, can sense you in all these ways. If he wished he could be at your side in just 9 seconds. In reality, he would probably run in the opposite direction. Misconceptions about wolves have led to their persecution and near extinction. Think of a wolf and immediately myths of werewolves and connections with evil spring to mind.

Through this book, I hope to take you beyond the myths and legends to a world only a lucky few have had the privilege to enter. A world where every day is a continuous battle for survival but where the wolf has come to realise (as most of us have) that the only thing that really matters is family.

Allow me now to give you an insight into this world; to reveal the breakthroughs, the setbacks and the understanding that both the wolves and we experienced, during our seven-year study into the dynamics of a captive wolf pack.

These wolves have touched our hearts in many ways. Now let me share with you their story.

Shaun's story – how it all began

My very first encounter with Canids happened when I was just a young boy growing up deep in the Norfolk countryside. The house in which we lived was surrounded by farmland, which in turn was edged by woodland.

At night the surrounding countryside became alive with a host of nocturnal creatures. Among them was a vixen and her young kits. To this day, I vividly remember the first time I met them.

As a young lad I was always compelled to sleep with my bedroom window wide open; even deep into the coldest winters. Crisp Northerly winds would carry the sounds of the nearby forest into my room and with the sounds came a familiar feeling of comfort and safety.

Night after night the voices of unseen creatures would provide me with my bedtime stories as I drifted into sleep. One memorable night, at the still very impressionable age of eight, I simply had to investigate the strange but familiar sounds that had awoken me. As I threw back the bedcovers and padded across my bedroom carpet, I was unaware that the adventure about to unfurl would be responsible for shaping the rest of my life.

From my window I could tell that the sounds were coming from restless horses in the meadow. In the silvery light offered by the full moon that had now climbed high in the sky, I could clearly see that the cause of their alarm was the red fox (vixen) and her kits, playing in the moonlight among the giant hooves of the horses.

I silently dared anyone not to admire the majesty that surrounded these creatures. Not satisfied with my vantage point, I climbed into my clothes and made my way, past the dog that slept beneath my bed, down to the back door where the boots were kept. Heart pounding with excitement, I stepped out into the dark and set off down the lane to the entrance of the forest.

I knew my way through the trees like the back of my hand and quickly found myself close to where the foxes were playing. I stayed with them for as long as I could stand the cold, which must have only been a few hours but, in that short time the foxes had cast their spell and, as my Native American teachers would remark many years later, it was on that night that I secretly signed nature's contract to work with animals.

Living in an area at a time when fox hunting still prevailed, I found myself, let us say 'frowned upon' by the local villagers. They could not understand why I spent so much time watching an animal that most of them considered to be vermin. These same people were later going to be even more confused when, upon leaving school, I took a job as a part time gamekeeper! They must have thought that their constant words of wisdom had finally led me to a new way of thinking and suddenly, I found myself on speaking terms with the villagers once more.

I was taken under the wing of my new employer and shown what it would take to become a good gamekeeper. However, my new-found popularity was to be short-lived, as was my new employment. After only a few weeks, my employer found out that the rabbit population he had worked so hard to catch was being fed to one of his arch rivals - the fox. I had been leaving the rabbits, scattered randomly around the woods near to where, as a young boy, I had seen the foxes playing.

To this day I am not sure if it was the fact that I had taken the rabbits or that I had broken his and the villagers trust that enraged him more. All I can say is the hours of delight spent watching this latest family generation grow and take their rightful place in the world were well worth the hours spent repaying the gamekeeper.

It was these early and somewhat eventful studies that would eventually lead me to North America, where I was able to both work with and study captive and wild wolves. My time with the foxes was to prove a valuable education and a foretaste of the future. But, it was in North America, under canvas, surrounded by at least 2-3 feet of snow, that I began to realise exactly what studying wolves would entail.

When we were not studying we would work, which involved the essential tasks of clearing snow from the roofs of the tents and collecting firewood to keep the stoves going. I tried to establish a routine of rising really early and completing my work as quickly as possible, then sleeping through until I heard the first wolves howling in the early hours of the morning. This was my cue to immediately jump from my sleeping bag, (which in itself was not an easy task).

The preparation for my trip to North America had been hasty (if there's one thing I learnt to my cost, it is that you just cannot rush packing, you need to check everything and then check it again). In said haste, I had packed a sleeping bag that belonged to a colleague. Unfortunately my colleague was a good deal smaller than I was, so his sleeping bag was somewhat snug! I spent many nights wrestling with this torturous bag and probably lost every bout.

When I finally managed to escape the clutches of the restrictive sleeping bag (by now thoroughly awake) I would make my way down to the enclosure where I would study the behaviour and record the sounds made by the wolves. Their howling echoed through the great forests, seeking out rival packs, desperate to locate each other's whereabouts. Despite popular belief, wolves will try to avoid conflict at all costs and howling is one of the most effective ways to achieve this.

Night after night I sat in the freezing temperatures, somehow managing to keep warm by digging a hole in the snow and then curling up in it, often beside the wolves themselves.

By placing my hands under my arms, I was able to keep them just warm enough to operate my recording equipment. I never grew tired

of listening to the wolves calling to one another or of their large feet padding by as I rested. To this day I still get the very same buzz every time I hear them.

Throughout the following day I would work with headphones on, analysing the many recordings I had made the previous night. My recording equipment was very basic and, on more than one occasion, I had to thaw out my tape machine in the sub zero temperatures, using my own body heat.

As I listened to the howling, I would try to pick out individual pack members through the distinctive sounds each wolf made. I began to identify the wolves by sound and to recognise the different types of howls they would use in order to communicate with one another. Listening to them in this way was effectively like listening to a language tape, though in this case, created by somewhat unconventional teachers.

I would sometimes allow myself a break from my studies to listen to the Indian biologists as they recounted stories of their ancestors and the close connections they had with the animals of the forests and plains. They told of how their tribal elders, who passed on from this world to the next, would be guided by a wolf. These animals were said to be past tribal members that had now taken the wolf's form. Even to this day, when signing land agreements, the Indians will take a dog along with them to witness the agreement, still believing it to possess the spirit of a tribal elder.

When their own people faced extinction, it was the wolf to whom they turned. By watching and learning from the resilience of this animal these people once more have become a proud nation. The pact the Indian people made with the wolf has never been broken. Even though modern man has made a mockery of the agreement in persecuting the wolf to near extinction, the wolf still honours the truce and remains to this day the only large carnivore, in their natural environment, not to attack man.

To the proud and noble people of North America, your wise words and patient teaching have inspired both myself and many others that have been privileged to work with you and call you friends,
 I thank you.

Jan's story

It's four in the morning and I'm drenched to the skin. The persistent rain has worked its way determinedly through three outer layers of clothing to my pyjamas and beyond. Perhaps the idea of keeping them on when I left my bed in haste was not so sensible after all! The rustling sounds I have been hearing are beginning to worry me. If Shaun has forgotten something and is on his way back, how come I can hear him at this distance?

Jan & Shaun walking in the woods

All around me is pitch-blackness. My thoughts turn to my fluffy duvet at home. It has never seemed more inviting. Another howl jolts me back to the present and my frozen fingers fumble with the tape recorder. The howls that issue forth mingle with Shaun's own howls and the marriage of sound travels through the darkened forest. A pause, only the sound of raindrops on leaves and my heart thumping. Suddenly, magically, the air is filled with strange and beautiful voices. The wolves, my reason for being here, have transformed my mood in an instant. I cannot help but smile. The unknown creature that I heard rustling earlier is perhaps my only witness...

When I first met Shaun I thought my future was more or less mapped out. I would work in an office until retirement, which would finance a nice car and finish the mortgage on my semi-detached home. My most exciting or dangerous decision would be which brand of orange juice to buy. Within weeks of meeting Shaun I could see this vision clouding, before it disappeared completely during the ensuing months.

My days off from work were no longer spent in clothes shops and coffee bars but sitting amongst bushes and trees watching an animal I knew very little about, the wolf. Not surprisingly, at first, I only had eyes for my new man but, as it dawned on me that he had a rare and special gift, his interactions with the wolves would hold my fascination more and more.

Within a few months I found myself so involved with Canids that it seemed a natural progression to work with the armed forces attack dogs. What I learned working with Shaun linked over to my work with the dogs and gave me much greater understanding. Before I knew it, my whole way of life had been transformed.

Armed with a new insight into the dynamics of wolf communication, I could see the true value of what Shaun was hoping to achieve and gave him my whole-hearted support. It's probably just as well I didn't know the many challenges that would face us, not least the financial hardship and sleep deprivation!

Once the press began to show an interest, we found ourselves giving interviews and this led to some memorable moments! A few years before I would have been horrified to be appearing on national breakfast television. Now, my heart filled with pride that so many others could appreciate Shaun's special talent.

When shopping in our regular local supermarket one day, we became uncomfortably aware that the youth stacking shelves was staring intently at Shaun. It was quite a relief when he shouted to his colleague 'it's the wolf man!'

Thankfully this and his ensuing comments were those of appreciation not, as we had originally thought, those of displeasure because of the strong odour of the wolves retained by our clothing.

No matter which television company we were filming with on any particular day, they all shared one thing in common, a disproportionate fear that the wolves would refuse to howl for them. Fortunately, they were never disappointed. Occasionally someone would get so carried away that they would find themselves joining in!

Seeing Shaun on television would never lose its novelty, even for the youngest family members. Our daughter, Kyra, would point at the screen and say 'Daddy!' It must have been quite confusing for her when he was sat next to her at the same time.

As to the wolves themselves, I have come to know them both as individuals and as members of a family not unlike my own. I only have to close my eyes to feel their presence. I can no longer imagine life without them, nor would I wish to. My world is their world.

Jan and Shaun

Introduction

It had been nearly one whole year since I was last with the Longleat wolves. Zeva and Lakota, the two pups, whom I had so reluctantly left at just a few days old, were now adults and had taken their rightful place within the pack's strict social hierarchy.

Watching Zeva moving through the shadows of the great trees that had once made up the vast Longleat forest made me realise just how long I had spent in the harsh, rugged mountains of Idaho. My mind wandered back to when she used to stumble around on oversized paws in a vain attempt to keep up with the adults. So many times I had found her and Lakota sleeping among the tall grass. They would both wake with a start, embarrassed that someone had managed to get this close to them undetected, then instantly reassure each other when they realised that it was only me.

Lakota himself was a miracle, having suffered a leg fracture as a result of his mum standing on him when just a few hours old. The keepers had taken a chance and removed him from the den, splinted the leg and then placed him back with his sister. The lack of mobility in the pups at that time and the familiar scent of the keepers who handled him throughout his absence, contributed greatly to his survival, along with one other important factor, the tiny wolf's own will to live. Never before have I known something so small to have such a big heart. As his strength grew, so did his nature. Lakota's strength comes from within. His name means peaceful person; never has a wolf been more aptly named.

The Longleat pack (like all other wolf packs) had suffered their own losses. As a new generation emerges, old ones must give way. Akaila died at the age of 15. He had led the pack for 11 years. Zeva and Lakota were to be Akaila's last offspring. Akaila means leader and up to the day he died, his family still looked to him as Alpha. There really is no better tribute to his memory.

Having not known Akaila very long, I cannot comment on his reign as leader, only on his reputation amongst those who knew him and the effect that his loss had on the remaining wolves. The pack's vulnerability was clearly evident but if they were to survive, they and I must now turn to a new leader.

CHAPTER 1

The Wolf Talk

The intricate language of the wolves has fascinated people for hundreds of years. Often depicted as magical or mystical, wolves have also been credited with telepathy and the power to shape-shift. Many of the myths and legends that surround the wolf connect them with evil. For centuries now, people said to have the power to take on the form of the wolf, only did so to fulfil their bloodthirsty cravings. Abandoning all of the wolves' natural behaviour, pack structure, avoidance and in-built fear of people, only the body form bears any resemblance to the wolf, the inner spirit displays mostly the characteristics of man. We do not need the form of the wolf to tell of our beast-like ways, it is written throughout our own history.

My teachers tell of a different form of shape-shifting, far removed from that of the half human, half wolf-like creature that howls by the light of a full moon. Their stories are much more in keeping with the animal's true nature and far more realistic than the creatures that help sell our movies and haunt our dreams.

For many years the very proud North American Indians have recognised the gifts that the wolves bring. Watching these animals hunt taught them to feed their families, by following their family bonds they raised their children and, harnessing their senses gave them an early warning to the approach of strangers.

According to legend, long ago an Indian woman, whilst out gathering wood for her tribal fires, fell upon a wolf pup. Alone and starving, the tiny animal seemed near to death. After looking around to try to find any signs of the young animal's family, she decided to take the pup back to her village and raise him amongst her own family. She gathered up the pup, wrapped him in her blanket and placed him in the basket.

Returning home, the woman took the young wolf pup into her tipi where it lived with her. She suckled the tiny creature on fresh warm milk and as it grew, brought it meat from the hunt. The wolf grew quickly and soon began to follow the woman as she travelled in search of firewood, food and water. Each morning, as the sun climbed in the sky, the woman and her young companion would travel down to the river to drink from its cool clear waters, watching their own reflections as the ripples settled.

When the sun began to set, the two of them would run and play among the trees of the forest, resting in the soft undergrowth as they listened to the sound of the creatures that shared their world, before returning home to sleep.

One morning, the woman and the wolf set off down to the river to drink. After satisfying their thirst, they walked back along the path that they had used the previous evening. The soft mud made it easy to see the two sets of prints that ran side by side. After a few paces the tracks that had shown both the wolf's prints and the woman's, now only showed two sets of wolf tracks.

Confused by what she saw, the woman went to see the old chief who told her that she had been given the wolf's gift in exchange for the tiny life that she had saved. He told her that she must run with her wolf family but she could always return to her tipi as she wished. That evening, the woman and the wolf went to the river to drink, as she sat beside the wolf looking into the water at her own reflection, it was not her body she saw sitting beside the pup but that of its she-wolf mother.

The woman continued to live among both her own people and her new wolf family, using the many gifts that she had been given in return for her act of kindness.

Such claims would seem to place the wolves' language far beyond our reaches yet perhaps this is not so. Through Indian legend, we discovered one very small group of people that were given the special gift of wolf communication.

During our time with our Native Indian teachers, we were told of many strange legends concerning the disappearance of braves who had been wounded in battle, women out gathering food or water and children out playing or 'counting coup'.

The word Coup is French and means 'blow'. The native plains Indians had a custom that was designed to humiliate, to test and deprive their enemy of valuable rest, with the stealth of the wolf, they would creep up, content to just touch the enemy with a stick, allowing him to live. The warriors called this 'Counting Coup'. Counting Coup was not only limited to sticks - a bow or even a bare hand was also used to great effect. Our modern societies seem to wage war on one another with only one intent, to kill each other.

Carrying sticks into battle, the warrior would run up to his enemy and tap or touch his opponent. The brave, after Counting Coup, would receive an eagle's feather for each successful Coup. If it was followed by a killing and scalping the brave would receive three eagles feathers. These acts of bravery, the mere touching of an armed opponent, were often recounted at their tribal fires, as the warriors told of their exploits. Any warrior that exaggerated their stories would face permanent shame from his fellow tribesmen.

Sometimes, people who disappeared would be lost for many years, but eventually they would be found, or would return to their own people, having been well fed and well looked after. Some spoke of how a wolf had come to them when they were near death, others of having crawled into a cave to escape the cold winds only to find it occupied by wolf pups. What they all shared was an initial fear that the wolves were waiting to feast upon their dead bodies but, they found that instead, the wolves brought food to sustain them and kept them warm throughout the long cold nights. When the people had grown strong on the fresh meat, the wolves would teach them to hunt. At night they would teach them the 'Wolf Talk', the wolves' own method of communicating with one another. The humans eventually returned to their own people, but thereafter they would always live on the outskirts of the villages, here they could best use the gift that had been given to them by the wolves and still remain close to their wolf family.

From these early days of wolf communication, we have now come further than ever before. So many times we have seen wolf packs that have been saturated with human dominance, people assuming this to be the safest way to interact with our fellow creatures, but what of the legends that had been told to us? Could a person truly be accepted as part of a pack of wolves?

Our Indian teachers believe that humans and wolves share the same eyes and that they themselves have been taught by their wolf brothers.

Over the last seven years my partner Jan and I have also allowed ourselves to be taught by these animals, living as they live. They have shown us more than we ever could have imagined…

CHAPTER 2

Running with the pack

The story of the wolves has been thoroughly documented over the years, with the emphasis often placed on their traditionally negative reputation. Nevertheless, it needs pointing out that wolves have an intricate family bond that bears a remarkable similarity to our own. I deliberately use the term family throughout this book to describe the wolf pack. This is partly because I personally have come to regard them as my own family but that is by no means the whole story.

Just as the human family has two leaders, one male and one female, so it is with wolves. The alphas are the protectors, the decision-makers and ultimately responsible for the well-being and discipline of their pack.

When I was with the wolves, I could instantly recognise the approach of my leader as distinct from that of any other pack member. In the pitch darkness, which was his element, he would come towards me, very sure and confident, on giant pads that would slap the ground as he trotted the last few feet to be by my side. Add to this the familiar rich scent that arose from feasting on the best quality foods and there was no mistaking him.

As the leader stood over me I would lower my body. Instantly his eyes would narrow, blink slightly and roll to one side, the subtlest of signs that meant I was allowed to greet my leader. I would turn my head up to him and lick at his muzzle. He would often raise his head towards the sky, making me stretch to continue my greeting and then, when I had reached him, he would turn his head to the side, making me work even harder for his affections before disappearing back into the darkness. This type of greeting was regularly used after the pack had eaten, reinforcing the bonds that had been stretched whilst at the kill.

The darkness was always an amazing time with the wolves, moving through the trees, along the snow covered pathways that had been used for many years by their ancestors before them. Now, saturated in the scent of the pack, they provided a safe passage as the pack (and I, as part of that family) travelled through our territory.

The leaders would dictate where we would scent, with each wolf carefully identifying their next rank up by its individual smell. As I held a mid-high rank within the pack my teacher was Reuben (the Beta male). At this stage I was not aware of the acute importance the wolves placed on this scent identification, but it would lead to a lesson that I would never forget.

Only after every tree stump, rock, bush and pathway had been reinforced with the entire pack's scent, was it time to announce to any rivals in the area that we were now ready to defend our territory and everything within it.

We formed the tight half circle that makes sending and receiving sound so much easier, then tilted our heads back in unison and called out into the night. All our eyes and ears are now trained on our leaders, awaiting their first howls.

Slowly my leader raised his head, pointing his powerful muzzle up into the clear night sky. Howling three times, each one slightly more intense than the previous, he paused briefly to scan the distance with his acute hearing. As his head turned in my direction I could feel his warm breath on my face. He began howling once more, this time joined by the alpha female. With my hands placed on the ground in front of me I could feel the ground vibrate from their calls.

My teacher Reuben, the beta male, had now joined the alpha pairing. I am guided (as are the rest of my pack mates) totally by my leaders, the focal point from which all-else stems. Carefully, overlapping the calls of my leaders that now filled the night, I blended my sound with theirs. My howl made up the middle ranks, using yips, yaps, barks, whines and howls. We helped create the illusion of larger numbers within the pack than there actually were.

After a few short breathtaking minutes, my leaders signalled to the remaining pack members and myself the end of the howl. As they stopped, so too did we. Moving towards our leaders we all closed in together, licking at each others muzzles, rubbing heads and bodies reinforcing the scents that bonded us together by smell.

Through the silence came the first calls of a reply from a neighbouring pack. We instinctively glided into a wider half circle to receive the rival pack's call, pressing our ears forward as each one of us tried to pick out the individual wolves that made up the other pack. As I listened I could clearly distinguish the rival alphas, both very low in tone.

However, the real key to understanding lay in the pauses between their howls, when they listened for the effect their calls were having on their challengers. The rival mid-ranking wolves used their howls as I had, making it very difficult to identify actual numbers but by this time each and every one of us was concentrating on one thing alone. There was only one beta rank howling, the female. The male's howl was absent from the pack. As the beta wolves rank extremely high, only answering to the alphas, this absence made the pack very vulnerable.

As the howl died out, we all bonded together, vying with each other to get close to the alphas. As we all approached our leaders there was a slight air of tension surrounding the wolves. (This type of behaviour is very common during territorial defence).

To my right, Zac has muzzled Reuben. I had heard the alpha growling as I approached the pack, clearly Reuben had needed a reminder of who was the boss. (The howl can be used sometimes to test high-ranking animals by continuing to call after the leaders have stopped).

The beta male's cry of submission had attracted the attention of the pack's omega. Occupying the lowest rank, the omega now performed one of its most important roles within the pack, that of peacemaker. The

scuffle between two high ranking animals could end in one or both being injured. Disabling the pack's hierarchy would weaken the entire family, placing them all in danger.

Simeon, our omega, knew his job well and was already between the two males. Reuben, having shown the correct respect to his alpha, could salvage some of the respect from the rest of the pack by standing over Simeon.

True to my own rank, I instantly went to Reuben and lowered myself to him. Accepting my gesture, he left the omega and walked off slowly, making me work slightly harder for his attention. Now joined by Simeon, the three of us bonded for several minutes before settling down to rest.

People always feel great sorrow for an omega rank, thinking them to be constantly bullied by the other wolves but their rank holds great importance within the pack.
We will never intentionally harm an omega, they are far too valuable, but their value, like any of us, is only justified by what happens from outside the wolves' territory. If this influence is missing, then the amount of attention shown to the omega will increase. In the past, I have witnessed quite severe injuries and bites to the flank and base of the tail. The base of the tail contains a scent gland that is as individual to the wolves as our fingerprints are to us. The omega is simply paying the price for doing their job in a pack that has no rivals.

Suddenly everyone froze. Off to our left, another voice echoed through the crisp night air. It was that of a lone wolf, cast out and roaming the buffer zones between packs, in search of the security that only a pack could offer. The missing rank revealed by our rival pack's howl could provide him with such an opportunity.

Over the many nights spent with the wolves I had sometimes heard outsiders join an established pack, but only when the pack was young or needed to increase numbers.

The lone wolf's calling did not concern us so, we did not reply. Over the next few nights we could hear him howling to the neighbouring wolves but no answer was given. Instead they continued trying to rally their beta, offering him a constant auditory beacon to find his way home.

We used the rallying howl to locate pack members at long distances. Every one of us could recognise our own pack's call and would reply to it instantly.

This howl has often been described as mournful, due to its poignant sound and the fact that it often comes at a time of death. For the wolves, pack survival comes at all costs and in their world, mourning the death of a family member must give way to restructuring the pack.

You could be forgiven for thinking you have just been reading about the untamed wilderness of North America, Canada or even parts of Europe, where wolves still roam free in their natural wild state. This is far from the reality - you have in fact just read the interactions between a captive pack of wolves and tape recordings of rival animals, the recording being designed to bond this resident family together. We are in the centre of England where the last wild wolf's howl died out several hundred years ago!

CHAPTER 3

Daisy's story - part 1

During our time with the wolves, all of them have touched us in different ways and every one of their stories holds a special meaning that will stay in our hearts forever. However, one wolf would defy all the odds, rewriting all of man's and God's laws. That wolf was Daisy.

Daisy's story begins on the 5th of May 1998. The lush grass of early spring already conceals the den entrance. Two tiny voices coming from within are the only things giving away any sign of life, as they suckle from their mother for the very first time in the safety of the darkness. A short distance away under the protective shade of a giant oak tree lays Daisy. Hidden from view, she carefully monitors the open countryside that borders the pack's territory.

The many years with her family and the loyal bond that has been reinforced between herself and the pup's mother over the last six months, are the only discipline she needs not to move. Watching her laying there in the tall grass at the base of the tree, it could be any other ordinary day, but her apparent calmness hides a fierce protective instinct that can be called upon in seconds.

Even with the distraction of the warm breeze that now blows through the trees, she has managed to hear the tiniest of sounds. After a few seconds the sound's whereabouts has been pinpointed. Rising to her feet she stretches, preparing her muscles for movement after the long period of motionless watching. Then carefully she makes her way to the den entrance, the origin of the sound.

Peering into the darkness Daisy is all too aware that, within this cramped environment, the two tiny wolves will be taught everything they need to survive amongst the adults.

She is desperate to see the pups but has already stayed at the den longer than she should. Reluctantly, she tears herself away and returns to her post.

Over the next few weeks the alpha female will carefully balance the teaching of her young, whilst reminding the adults of the lessons that they themselves would have learnt as pups. Long before the pups take their first wary steps from the den, they will have already become aware of their family through their scent.

However, for the first few weeks of the pup's lives they see, hear and smell only their mother. This is her time. Here, deep below ground in a carefully made birthing chamber, that she would have spent many days making and testing, she suckles her young and regulates their temperature. She nurtures them, safe in the knowledge that as they grow, the shallow bowl she has dug out and placed them in will prevent them from wandering down the narrow tunnel to meet her.

Unlike their wild brothers, captive wolves have very few predators, with most casualties arising from their mother standing or rolling on them as she enters or leaves the den. Hundreds of years of instinct have taught her this is the time that both she and the pups are most at risk.

Daisy shuffles uneasily. Her ears alone have told her of the presence of the leader. The leader is about to emerge, scratching and clawing her way up the narrow passage towards the entrance of the den. Daisy stands motionless before her.

The Alpha shakes the dust from her fur. Daisy lowers her body respectfully. The lack of contact during her leader's confinement and the new scent she now brings with her do not distract Daisy from showing the correct response to a dominant animal. Years of experience have taught Daisy exactly how to act in the presence of her leaders and following her show of respect, she is quickly given permission to greet the pup's mother.

Unable to contain her excitement any longer, Daisy frantically licks at the alpha's muzzle for a first taste of the pups' scent, carried from the mother's attentive grooming and licking to stimulate their toilet.

As the young wolves grow over the next few weeks, their mother's involvement will be reduced to suckling them and monitoring their progress as they develop into adulthood. Daisy will take on the role of their nanny, their protector and teacher; this very first introduction by smell begins their unique bond.

It is now mid April and the pups are two weeks old. The early summer sun continues to grow in strength and from the den, small scuffles can be heard as the young wolves begin to discover the importance of rank. The increase in activity has brought the ever-watchful Daisy closer to the entrance of the den.

Her patience will soon be rewarded as their mother spends less and less time below ground with her pups.

The once blind and helpless young wolves slowly make their way down the dark passage that has been their security now for over three and a half weeks. Drawn to the warm sunlight and a familiar scent that has so often been brought to them on their mother's fur, the two tiny figures finally appear, their bright blue eyes squinting in the summer sunlight.

Daisy moves slowly towards the young wolves, using her body to shade them as she licks at her new charges. Just as their mother has taught them, the two pups immediately roll over to expose their vulnerable light undersides.

For nearly four weeks Daisy has watched and waited above ground for the two bundles of fur that now lay at her feet, now she must guide them to adulthood. She will need all the bonding and trust these first few precious moments will provide, if she is to succeed.

By now the summer sun is very strong and small heat waves have begun to appear. The heat of the day quickly drains the young wolves of their energy. Where they once retired to the cool shade of the den, they now seek out the shade of the giant trees.

Their adventures may now take them anything up to a mile from the safety of their place of birth and shade is not the only thing these trees provide. Deep among the roots and hidden from view, small holes have been made to accommodate the young wolves should danger appear. Only two or three feet below the ground they offer amazing protection for any tiny wolf that may become separated from the pack during confusion. Both pups would have already been shown where to find these safe havens by Daisy. She would have also clearly marked their whereabouts with her own familiar scent, making them easy to locate quickly in times of danger.

Watching the two tiny shapes as they rest between the outstretched legs of their guardian, it suddenly all becomes so clear. Everything the young wolves have been taught is now beginning to make sense. They have been given the greatest lesson of all, that of survival.

It is an ongoing lesson, woven into the everyday lives of their own family and passed on to each new generation. Even among animals that speak with one voice, nothing is left to chance. Neither luck nor

instinct have guided the pups to the scent of the nanny they now lie beside, it is the patient teaching of many generations of wolves over hundreds of years that guides them.

The lessons always remain the same, only their teachers may change. All that has been needed from Daisy and the pup's mother is to remind the adult wolves of their own time as youngsters.

As for myself, in beginning to understand the simplicity of these most misunderstood of all of nature's creatures and the ways they are taught to survive, my thoughts are drawn to the uncertain future of mankind.

Late afternoon and the now cooling air have slowly brought the three figures from their resting-place. Daisy rises and stretches, in her customary way but this time she is mimicked by the two young wolves at her side. They have also discovered the importance of preparing their muscles after the long rest. This act has not been deliberately taught by Daisy but has been learnt by association; watching and learning, *(something we would do well to remember as an aid to training our domestic dogs).*

The two tiny pups are of the same gender, so the small bouts of squabbling among them helps to reveal the importance of defending that which is theirs. Daisy begins the pup's teaching with a raven's feather that has floated down from a nest lodged high in the trees. Her play bows and dancing from side to side now shows the young wolves one of the many meanings that accompany this type of behaviour, the all important lesson of hunting and how to catch food. The feather is left hanging tantalisingly from one side of her mouth. This tells the pups that it is fair game; if she did not want them to take it she would seal it in her mouth and growl at them when they tried to remove it. After a brief game of tug-of-war, the feather is released for them to play with among themselves. Now Daisy watches carefully to determine who is the more dominant pup.

These early indications of dominance will help place the pups within the pack's rank structure. After a few seconds it becomes clear that 'One Crop' is the slightly more dominant of the pair. Daisy has seen enough for today and moves in to take the feather. At this stage she removes it with little resistance from the two pups, but over the next few days this feather will be replaced by food from the kill, which they will have to be prepared to defend.

By now the two pups have been introduced to the remaining adults who, led by the alpha pair, are returning from the kill. Both Daisy and the young wolves rush forward to meet them.

The pup's mother calls them away to suckle, whilst Daisy begs food from the other adults. The wolf family is very co-operative, with their social skills among the most highly developed in the animal kingdom.

Today they have returned with a calf's leg, which Daisy quickly grabs. With her food secured she heads for where the pup's mother is suckling her youngsters, knowing that they will look for her as soon as they have finished.

Daisy begins to feed from the bone, carefully keeping her eyes trained on her leader as she does so. Even the pup's nanny must still obey pack rules.

The pups have taken their nourishment and make their way towards Daisy. This prompts her to stop eating and stare straight at them, her eyes opened wide.

This is a far cry from the usual softness that she shows towards them. They have not seen the warning signs and continue to move closer. Now she lets out a low growl, but still the pups are unaware of her intentions. Finally Daisy stands up, lowers her head and splays her ears.

Her facial expression now matches her growl in intensity, her teeth are bared and her tongue protrudes through them. The message is now loud and clear, she is defending her food.

Chastened, the two pups move away and rejoin the remainder of the pack. Their lesson may seem harsh, but from this encounter and many more like it, they will slowly learn how to defend their own food from others, probably even from Daisy herself.

In the coming weeks, such lessons will be of great importance to One Crop and his brother. When you are at the kill, surrounded by the adult wolves with a window of only a few inches in which you can feed, the importance of food defence becomes all too clear.

The pups are now three months old, Daisy and the rest of their pack continue to guide them towards adulthood.

Sadly, this is where I must leave them. My research for Wolf Pack Management will now take me back to North America. Over the many months I have lived alongside these wolves, they have taught me far more than they have taught the two pups. It's hard to imagine spending even one night without them.

4

Return to North America

Looking through the giant trees the lush green vegetation, that in a few short months would be under three to four feet of snow, now moved in the light breeze as it soaked up the warm sun. The breathtaking wilderness stretched far beyond the naked eye.

The air smelt fresh and clean with the absence of traffic fumes, a clarity that was shared by the moss growing on the side of the trees. Standing there, surrounded by such untouched beauty, it is easy to see why the wolves have chosen to call this home.

After storing away my equipment in the tented accommodation, I could not resist a walk in the brilliant sunshine. I followed one of the many paths that ran through the great forest. Disturbing a grey owl, I wondered how many more creatures' eyes were on me as I moved through the trees.

The forest plays host to a variety of mammals and birds, fox, deer, mouse; all too shy to show themselves to me, but I could feel their eyes were close by, using the shadows of the trees to remain undetected. I rested by a tree, listening to the forest's occupants calling to one another. With the thought of these many eyes on me, I recalled a near encounter between one of the students working with us at the time - and a mountain lion…

During the winter a number of students had come to study the wolves. After only a few days students are encouraged to form their own routines for food and work around the camp.

One of the girls decided to incorporate a fitness routine into her daily duties. As she enjoyed jogging, each morning and night she would travel down the track to the bottom of the road and back, a distance of some three to four miles.

After three weeks, one of the biologists and I were returning from collecting food for the wolves from the nearby town, when my teacher spotted the girl's fresh tracks in the new falling of snow. We travelled about a mile up the track, where her prints were joined by those of a large cat. My teacher informed me that they were the tracks of a mountain lion. The paw prints matched, stride for stride, those of the young girl; trailing her up the track.

We immediately jumped into the vehicle and began up the trail, arriving at camp just as the young girl was stretching after her run. After explaining to her that she had acquired a running partner, we walked back down to where we had last seen the lion's tracks.

It turned out that the animal had followed her to within 150 metres of camp, resting, watching her movements as she jogged by unaware that she was being watched.

From that day on the girl's exercise routine stopped. Not wishing to test the mountain lion's speed over a mile or so, she felt this

was the safest compromise.

I made my way back to camp to prepare for the following day. We had an early start and an intense week of work ahead. I decided that an early night's sleep would be in order. Besides, the wolves calling as darkness fell would be sure to get me up. I could never resist listening to them well into the early hours; there was no reason to believe that I would stop now.

During my time with my Native American teachers, I would constantly be reminded of the special bond they had with their fellow animals and their abilities to read the creatures that share their world. Never was this more evident than when we were working close to the bears.

It was on these occasions that I came to realise some of my limitations and just how little I really knew of the world outside my wolf family. In spite of all my in-depth lessons, from anti-bear attack drills, to how my reactions could save my life, nothing could prepare me for my first wild bear encounter.

There are no fences to hide behind, no vehicles to run to, only a few metres of open ground that, if it chose to, the bear could cover in seconds.

This open ground however was all my teachers needed, together with knowledge of the wilderness that had been passed onto them by their ancestors for thousands of years.

As the bears approached I stuck close to my teachers. I watched their faces for the slightest changes as they read the bears' intentions and listened attentively to every word they spoke, as they calmly reeled off the history between the bears and their own people, sometimes with a window of only a few metres.

Often the bears would pass us by without conflict but on the rare occasions, when we needed to give ground to them, we would move calmly away and allow them to pass by.

To my teachers the bear has always symbolised all that is great and powerful within the wilderness. They once told to me a story of a bear that had been wounded in the back by hunters. Seeking the most remote and inaccessible place, the bear climbed the tallest mountain it could find. Still the hunters followed the bear, chasing it right into the sky.

The chase is still said to go on today. 'The Great Bear' - Ursa Major, can be seen running across the sky, with the four cup stars of the Big Dipper (the hunters) behind him.

Every Autumn, when the sun has set, the bear is said to run upside down, spilling blood from the wound on its back onto the Autumn leaves below and turning them red.

Living in the midst of the North American wilderness, I was deeply moved by the vast knowledge revealed by both the wolves and my human companions, with regard to the animals that shared their territory.

I soon realised that showing these animals the respect they deserved was just as important as showing respect to my alpha in the wolf pack.

Often inevitably, my thoughts would turn to home and in particular to Daisy and her young charges' education. She would by now be teaching them the same valuable lessons I myself was learning hundreds of miles away from them.

Returning to camp one day, I received word from home. Jan had instinctively known that my thoughts would be with the wolves and was well aware of my need to hear how they were faring.

Sadly, after reading only a few short lines, I was distressed to learn that Macha (the pup's mother) had died shortly after I left. I finished reading the letter but was unable to absorb anything further.

Macha had been the alpha female for as long as I could remember. She had mothered Zeva, Lakota and the two pups I had left behind. In my absence they must elect a new leader; I wondered if it would be Daisy.

Late that night the news of Macha's death would not leave my thoughts. Far from the pack, I was without the luxury of howling with them, calling for her to return. This howling, although not mournful, always seemed to help me deal with the death of a family member. I guess that was still the human nature in me, burning somewhere deep inside.

I stepped outside of my tent and the crisp evening air stung the back of my throat as I tried to choke back my sadness. Slowly I picked my way down through the trees towards the wolves' enclosure. Even though this was not my pack I simply had to howl. I stopped short of the trees that surrounded the wolves' territory, sat down and cupped my hands over my mouth.

Slowly, I began to howl for my alpha. Long drawn out notes echoed through the still night air, all my emotions tied up in every sound.

It can only have been a few seconds before my howling brought the first replies back to me. From deep within the forest, a lone wolf desperate to find a mate had answered my cries. I listened as she carefully howled and then moved position before howling again, trying to make it as difficult as she possibly could for neighbouring packs to pinpoint her whereabouts. As she finished howling the resident pack began, announcing their territorial claim.

In those brief moments I had said good-bye to my leader in the best way I knew how. Long into the night I could hear the wolves calling to each other and once, very briefly, in the mysterious world between sleep and wakening, I thought I heard the familiar howl of Macha. Maybe I did.

All too soon winter was upon us. Layers of snow now covered the ground and the bears had long since sought shelter in their underground homes.

My regular letters from home told me that Daisy had indeed become the new alpha female and successfully pair-bonded with Fang, the alpha male. This would be Daisy's first chance to pass on her genes to the next generation.

No wolf was more deserving of such an honour. She had lived in the shadow of Macha for many years, climbing with her as she moved up through the ranks.

Macha's death, shortly after the birth of her pups, had provided Daisy with a chance to bring up the young wolves as their mother. The help she would have recruited at this time would soon provide the same care to her own young, along with all the knowledge she would have learnt from her own leader.

Remembering my own teacher's words; 'The lessons never change, only the teachers,' brought a huge smile to my face that was instantly questioned by those same people.

My reply was simple. 'You wouldn't believe me if I told you!'

My time in North America was over. Having said my good-byes to the wolves and my colleagues, we began the long trip to the airport. One of my teachers had offered to drive me and so the long journey was pleasantly broken up with more stories of his people's history.

Just as two brothers would, we hugged each other good-bye, safe in the knowledge that we would never be very far from each other's thoughts.

C H A P T E R 5

Return to Longleat

Our first thoughts were of Daisy's welfare. At least one tiny body was lying stillborn beside her and she was clearly in distress. Anxious keepers now had to move quickly if they were going to save Daisy.

She was removed from the pack and rushed to the veterinary surgery where, during the medical examination by the vet, it was discovered that one tiny pup had caused an obstruction, with all of the remaining pups also dead.

If any other wolf had left with such complications I would have seriously doubted the possibility of their return. However this was no ordinary wolf, this was Daisy.

Greatly assisted by the keepers and staff that cared for her welfare she returned, against all the odds, to once more lead the pack that she has been such a part of now for fifteen years.

Sadly the only drawback suffered, in an otherwise complete return to her old self, was the fact that whilst under anaesthetic the decision had been made to sterilise Daisy for her own safety.

These types of decisions are never easy to make, particularly when they effect the wolf's hierarchy so much, but the animal's welfare takes top priority.

In the wild, she would have almost certainly died from such complications and the pack would have elected a new alpha. Daisy's return now offered a whole new challenge for the pack. They now had an alpha female who was unable to produce pups.

1.30 a.m., not a breath of wind could be felt and no sounds could be heard. Overhead the sky was clear, all that could be seen was the millions of stars. My eyes were drawn to the familiar Great Bear closely followed by the four Hunters, looking down on me as they had done so many nights before.

Slowly, I made my way down the valley to the small copse that overlooked the wolves' territory. I made myself comfortable under the weary branches of an old hollow tree. I had sat there on many occasions watching for the wolves, under the keen eyes of a pair of tawny owls that returned every year to nest in one of its hollow boughs. The time had come to call to the wolves.

The still night air was suddenly broken by Jan's voice coming over the radio to tell me they were ready to go. The two speakers sited on the roof of the vehicle now filled the air with our challenge.

From where I was sitting I could only just make out the ghostly figures of the wolves as they moved in and out of the shadows, rallying the pack with a series of high pitch whimpers to a position from which they could defend. Sure enough, within seconds they began howling to repel the challenge.

The still night air provided me with an ideal chance to pick out the sounds of individual wolves. Although lacking a little in confidence, they were still together and prepared to defend.

The only rank that was under threat was that of alpha female. Daisy's vulnerability was evident in her howl and the rest of her pack knew it. Despite being a little shaky, Daisy held her own and led her pack against our challenge. Now I needed to see how she would respond to a challenge made to her alone.

Using recordings of a lone wolf matching Daisy's rank should instantly get a reaction from her.

Motionless and with my eyes trained on the clearing where I had last seen the wolves, I waited for Daisy to reply to the solitary sound that now filled the air. For what seemed like a lifetime but was in reality only a few minutes, I sat there willing her to respond with all my being. There was nothing but silence. I moved the voice of the lone wolf forwards; taking up the ground that had not been defended. We called once more but still there was no response.

In those few short moments, Daisy's silence had confirmed my suspicions. As I made my way back up the valley to where the team was positioned, the look on their faces mirrored my own inner feelings.

Over the next few days I carefully monitored Daisy's progress within the pack, noting her interactions, her leadership of the pack and how well she defended her food.

Based on these findings, both myself and the rest of the team could only conclude that the best course of action for the pack as a whole and more importantly Daisy, would be to attempt to persuade her to accept a lower rank.

The breeding season approached and the added pressure this entailed would do Daisy no favours at all. (This would have applied to any wolf of her age, sterile or not).

In the wild, all such aspects of the wolf's world would be taken care of naturally using the delicate balance between elements from inside and outside the pack.

In a captive environment, by our careful intervention, not only can we maintain the wolves' own behavioural methods, we can also apply the natural pressure that is so important in maintaining pack harmony, at a time when it is needed most. Moving Daisy to a lower rank clearly shows the importance of the effect that a rival pack has on our resident wolves.

My only concern was the possibility of dispersal. This occurs when an animal is not prepared to accept a lower rank and is forced to leave. Once again this is where nature's delicate balance comes in.

The natural dispersal of wolves in the wild greatly assists their bloodlines. It will also play an important part a little later with our own captive packs breeding programmes. At the moment however, it must be avoided at all costs.

Natural dispersal can be bypassed in some situations by carefully monitoring the wolves' feeding routines and the correct amount of complete rival packs that occupy neighbouring territories.

It's now almost midnight and the constant rain has finally worked its way through to my underwear!

Driven on by the knowledge that these early stages are so

important, I prepare to challenge the pack once more. Their reply, as it has
so many times before, quickly makes me forget just how much rainfall
there has been, only the thick layer of mud beneath my feet serves as a
brief reminder. Even the harsh weather does not detract from the
excitement and sense of belonging I feel each time they howl.

As the pack finishes its response I begin the call from our lone
wolf. Again there is no reply from Daisy, but in the distance the faint
sound of pack interaction can be heard. The pack's restructuring has
begun.

From a distance I can see the team vehicle, easily recognisable as it has
only one headlight working! I have spent the last of our money on
batteries for the sound equipment used to communicate with the wolves.

Anyone working with animals will understand that total
commitment to those in your care becomes a way of life. Sadly, it is not a
view shared by our local constabulary when they are trying to enforce the
law, as I have discovered on more than one occasion on my journey home
from the wolves!

Gazing down at my watch tells me that it is indeed time for the
relief shift. I am not sure if it is the look on my face or the nasty
squelching sound that I make as I climb into the vehicle but Jan is already
pouring me a welcome hot cup of coffee.

After exchanging our thoughts of the night's activities she
prepares to settle down for the rest of the day.

It is vitally important to have someone on hand at all times.
When the wolves decide to begin their own challenges or re-organisation,
we need to be there to respond. They have to feel that the neighbouring
territories are constantly occupied by rival packs of wolves.

To create this illusion the recordings of the wolves must be as
authentic as possible. Challenging or defending, the success of the
management programme depends on the realism that our tapes can
provide.

Sometimes, this realism proved to be a little too authentic, not to
the wolves, but to the local fishermen that used to fish at night on the
Leat (the waterway running through Longleat Park from which it gains its
name.)

On one particular night, Jan and I prepared to play rival packs to the wolves. Each recording had its own territory to occupy, defend and challenge from. By this stage, we had increased the pressure on the wolves to encourage the final part of their role reversal.

As we set up the equipment, Jan commented on all the lights used by the fishermen along the banks to see their lines and asked if maybe we should go to them and let them know what was now about to happen.

Confidence in the fishermen's knowledge that wolves lived in the park close to where they sat, and put off by the thought of the long walk down to where they were, greatly influenced my reply.

'It's fine, they've probably heard the wolves howling hundreds of times before'.

Satisfied with my answer, Jan continued to wire up the equipment before moving into position. After playing the tapes and getting the satisfactory response from our wolves, we were both drawn to the noise that now seemed to come from the fishermen's car park.

Looking down the hill to where they had once sat, all that could be seen were the many lamps now moving quickly along the bank towards their cars.

Turning to Jan, I naively and in true Sherlock Holmes style, deduced that they must have finished. It was not until the next morning that I discovered the real reason for their hasty departure.

In one way my faith in the fishermen's knowledge of the wolves' whereabouts was correct and in fact their calling had not bothered them. It had been the fact that they had heard so many of them and all from different areas that they thought the wolves were loose, causing them to abandon their night's activities and return to their homes, something I feel they may never forgive me for.

I hugged Jan good-bye as she settled down for the day and I headed for home, with eager thoughts of the dinner she had prepared for me.

The next day, I briefly called in on Jan to find out what had happened during the early hours of the morning (another good time when wolves are most active). She too confirmed that the sound of increased pack interaction could be heard following the howl.

I made my way down to the wolves; the time had now come to give further consideration to feeding routines.

The wolves' feeding routine consisted in this case of two main elements, feeding whole carcasses and a 'feast and famine' diet. Feeding whole carcasses enables the wolves to naturally define their own rank structure, with lower ranking animals eating lower quality foods than high ranking ones. This gives the advantage to dominant animals over subservient ones without conflict.

The quality of food among captive animals is such that no animal suffers as a result of this type of feeding and the benefits that derive from it are unquestionable.

The feast and famine diet mirrors the wolves' natural feeding habits. The wild wolves' hunting success rate is roughly one kill for ten attempts (depending on food availability and time of year) which means that whilst they hunt most of the time, they rarely actually make a kill.

Co-operative hunting prior to feeding, again cements the wolves' natural bonds, giving them time between feeding to reinforce pack structure.

As the wolves' food was brought in to them, I began to watch for their reaction; not just to the prospect of eating but more importantly, their reaction to one another. Using one large piece of food rather than several pieces would now provide the pack with the opportunity to firstly create and then maintain restructuring.

To an outsider there may appear to be no order whatsoever in the way wolves feed, frantically ripping into a carcass en masse. In fact, it is a carefully orchestrated process in which every wolf has its own set position to feed from, governed by rank.

Today, I could tell from watching the wolves eating that the outside influences were steadily weaving their magic. It would not be long before we would hear this evidence reflected in their calls. The wolf that we hoped would take Daisy's place as alpha female was Zeva.

Once, under the care of her nanny, Zeva would have been taught all the behaviour and communication she needed for pack survival. Now she would be given the chance to use it. Ironically Zeva's nanny had been Daisy herself!

The next two nights brought little change from the wolves or the weather, though there was an intensity about the interactions between pack members after the lone wolf had called.

Patience was called for and we decided our best option was to stay on site, with our vehicle offering some protection against the inclement weather. One of us would listen whilst the other slept.

It was during the early hours of the morning on the fifth night that Zeva responded to recordings of lone wolves with her first defence as alpha female.

We reacted swiftly by playing the rival pack's howl to help the wolves and ourselves confirm the change in ranks. The short time between us issuing our challenge and the pack replying seemed interminable. Both Jan and myself stood, hardly daring to breathe, and then in a moment of pure magic that will stay with us for the rest of our lives, Zeva's howl rang out across the valley, confirming her new alpha status. Behind her, the entire remaining pack could be heard; even Daisy's howl was clearly evident as she backed her new leader.

Throughout the night the pack issued their own series of challenges, announcing to any rival packs that they had once more become a complete family.

The only sounds now absent were those of the recordings of the lone wolves. As if in the wild, we had to maintain authentic conditions for our wolves. With their possible pack acceptance rejected, the vacancy having been filled from within, they must now take care not to alert complete packs of their whereabouts.

Who would have thought that, such a small amount of communication could mean so much to so many animals, but this is the way of nature, when the battle for survival takes place on a daily basis.

Like other creatures, wolves do nothing just for fun and, as we can now begin to appreciate, details that mean very little to ourselves could make all the difference to the wolves in our care.

Over the next few months I watched the pair bond between Zeva and Fang, the alpha male grow.

But what of Daisy? As the breeding season fast approached, would she be able to write another chapter in her remarkable diary of life and once more guide the next generation of Longleat wolves to adulthood? We would have to wait and see.

CHAPTER 6

Living with the pack

Dawn, always my favourite time with the wolves. To my rear, stretching far beyond the naked eye, was Dartmoor. One by one breaking through the thin layer of mist that still cloaked the ground, the five strong pack of wolves came to investigate the strange new odour that now filled their territory. The distinctive sickly smell of human; a combination of body sprays, boot polish and a wide variety of smells brought to them from the outside world, mixed with at least three other wolf pack's scent still clinging to my clothing.

Zac, the alpha male, was the first to show any interest. We began to communicate from a distance, meeting each other's gaze just long enough to identify each other's intentions. His eyes fixed on me, wide and challenging, with no movement from the head.

The only sound to an otherwise silent exchange was the high pitched whimper with which he now called the remaining pack members to his side.

With his family's support now clearly evident, it was time for him to push his advantage. He came towards me, using a straight and direct line, to inform me of his intentions. I lowered my head and stepped to one side, accepting his authority.

This simple exchange happened so quickly and with such subtle body language that, from the outside, no one would have ever known we had even spoken a word.

This is one of the many reasons why wolves are often credited with mystical powers and that of telepathy.

In those few short moments, I had been told that my acceptance was not going to be instant. This was the perfect situation for what I had to do.

Our introduction of a rival pack's howls would this time be for an entirely different reason from that of the outside challenge to the Longleat wolves.

This time they would be used to allow my way into the wolf pack, creating the all-important gap that must be opened before an outsider can be accepted into the resident pack.

We began howling to the pack, using recordings of large numbers of wolves, initially at a distance and taking great care not to apply too much pressure too soon.

Introducing rival packs to wolves is very effective but, it can also be extremely dangerous; in the wild it could easily disperse wild wolves from their territory. However in captivity, there is nowhere for them to go so the consequences could be disastrous.

Now, having had the chance to study the wolves, I could clearly identify that the vulnerable area for the pack was the middle ranks. That would be the niche that I would try to occupy.

I have sometimes been asked whether I thought the wolves perceived me as human or wolf and a reporter once asked my partner Jan the same question in an interview. I can recall her reply to this day.

'Shaun has always lived somewhere between the wolf's world and ours but, if you ask me what percentage of their world he occupies then I have no comment.'

My own reply would be that the wolves do not see me as either wolf or human, rather they regard me as someone that holds a rank within their pack; a rank that must first be gained and then defended and maintained, sometimes many times a day.

Using the sounds of rival packs, we began to create a gap within the resident pack; using large numbers of rival wolves quickly identifies problem areas among the pack's ranks where they are weakest but again, using these large numbers of wolves can be extremely hazardous. This is why we use our recordings at great distances away from the animals, ensuring that the correct amount of pressure is applied. It also allows us to move slightly closer when we need to take up ground from the wolves, to emphasise the rival pack's intent if the resident pack is not strengthened.

Once a gap had appeared the wolves' vulnerability was clearly evident in their replies to our challenges. It was time for me to make my attempt to join their family.

When the wolves began looking for a lifeline it came in the form of a lone wolf, in this case a male lone wolf. Male wolves are usually higher in defensive qualities than females and as they needed to strengthen their numbers to keep rival wolves at bay, what better candidate than an adult male, complete with all the defensive qualities they now so greatly needed?

I had made sure that this animal fitted their exact requirements. As the tension mounted and the rival packs moved ever closer, I stayed close to the boundary of my new pack's territory, gradually beginning to use my own howl to help strengthen their territorial battle.

Throughout the next few nights I constantly listened for the rival wolves to challenge, ever ready to join in with the resident wolves' reply. Missing a chance to help the pack defend could result in one of the many lone wolves (who also await their chance to rejoin or to start their own families) making their own campaigns to add strength to a vulnerable pack.

If I was to succeed in my quest, then the challenge of these nomads, that also live close by in the territory around and between the packs, must be dealt with before I could earn the right to once more become part of a secure pack.

My howl within the group would be used to create numbers. Mid ranking wolves will use yips, yaps, barks, whines, howls, growls; anything to give the illusion that there are more wolves in the pack than there actually are. The more often we defended our territory, the more the wolves came to rely on my presence to see off the challenge, until eventually we were howling as one pack. At that point the rival wolves ended their threat.

Many times throughout the night I would visit with the pack, announcing my arrival to them by sound. Their rallying replies that echoed back to me through the darkness of the trees were of great comfort, telling me that I was welcome among their pack.

Having asked permission to greet individual members of the wolves' hierarchy by lowering myself and allowing them to identify me by scent, I would then be given permission to exchange greetings with pack members. Picking my way through the rank structure to the point when it was my turn to show dominance and gain the trust of the wolves that held a lower position than mine. I would give and take the respect that my mid-rank demanded.

Through the wire of the enclosure I would interact with my new family, playing, resting, scenting and defending before once more leaving them to check for any fresh scent that may have been left by a rival lone wolf close to my new boundary. It would not be long now before I would not have to leave their security. It was becoming harder and harder for me to drag myself away from the pack.

Staying with them longer each time, throughout the night it was now time for me to take my place inside the pack. Having created and accepted my position, I must now be prepared to defend it. Walking into that enclosure for the first time reminded me greatly of my feelings during the very first encounter I had with wild bears. This was the moment of truth.

The wolves greeted me as they would one of their own, my submissive stance that was now familiar to the pack's hierarchy, reinforcing my position. One by one they identified my scent, before carefully blending it with their own by rubbing themselves against me.

The wolves have good reason for this behaviour. Most people are aware that wolves and dogs 'see' mostly without the use of colour. Their visual world is largely made up of shades of grey. However, it is not only their vision that is grey, the territory they occupy is also effectively 'colourless' in terms of scent as the pack's smell overlays all.

After a few short days and nights living with the wolves you discover senses you never knew you had. Everything within the wolves' homeland is laced in their scent, each individual pack member, the tree stumps and the trails that provide safe passage through their territory. They can instantly recognise a stranger's odour.

A story once told to me by my Native American teachers was of a woman who had been hurt and had fallen behind her travelling people. Starving, she came upon a wolf's den and crawled inside. She lay close to the pups for warmth. At first the adults were suspicious and afraid of her but they still returned every day to bring food for their young, which the woman shared.

Eventually she grew strong enough to snare rabbits and help with the hunt. She stayed with the pack for many years. Then one day the oldest wolf smelt humans coming and strangely, so too did the woman. They were her own people and she knew she must return to them. The woman moved towards them very slowly because she found their smell was so strong it made her sick.

But she did not come alone; she brought with her the skills she had learnt from the wolf people. By listening to the wolf talk at night and with the benefit of her sensitive nose, she could predict the weather far in advance and alert the villagers when game or humans were close by.

She lived out the rest of her life on the outskirts of the village through her own choosing, where she could simultaneously stay with her own people and be close to her wolf family.

My own feelings only serve to confirm what the woman's story told. As Jan arrived to bring me food, passing it through into the pack's enclosure, I slowly began to recognise the wolves' reaction when they sensed her arrival through scent. I immediately began to raise my head slightly skywards, creating an open airway to give my own sense a fighting chance against the wolves' acute sense of smell. Desperately sniffing the air, I attempted to identify her. My olfactory sense was nowhere near as highly-developed as that of the wolves but I slowly began to recognise her scent as she approached.

As my own smell slowly began to merge with that of the pack, it became easier to identify the outside world. The days and nights I spent with my wolf family all too quickly turned into months. The deaths and injuries, old age and constant testing had now brought me through the ranks to beta male. I had come through my everyday battles, learning each wolf's position.

Regrettably I had been taught by the old beta male for only a few short weeks when he died, leaving a big gap in my education.

Once more as it had so many times before, the pack was forced to restructure. We had been calling for the dead beta now for three days, but no replies came. The howl used at such times sounds almost mournful and has often given the illusion to the outside world that the pack may actually mourn the death of a family member. In truth we are trying to identify their whereabouts. From their reply we can tell if they are injured, trapped, returning, or have left the pack for the purpose of starting their own family. If no reply comes then we must elect a new pack member to fill the missing position.

Once the pack calls, (as we can now see) neighbouring packs and lone wolves quickly learn that a pack is not at full strength. For rivals, it is a chance to expand their territory, which in turn could mean more food and a greater chance of survival.

For lone wolves, (animals who have been ousted or have simply left of their own accord and who live on the fringes of the packs) this is a chance to rejoin the security that a pack provides.

Using our recordings, the team once more began to apply pressure from rival packs keeping ever alert to the vulnerability of the territory. At the same time we employed the sounds of two lone wolves, played from different locations around the pack.

To show the wolves that I was worthy of taking on the beta rank I first had to see off the challenge from these wolves by announcing to them that I was prepared to fill the vacant position. My howl was strong and full of confidence telling any would-be challengers that I was in prime condition and free from illness.

Over the next few nights I filled the air with my calls, never letting the outsiders rest, constantly ready to defend. Following every successful howl I would immediately reinforce my position within the pack, especially with my alpha. Like a child desperate to make a good impression on new friends, I never missed an opportunity to convince him and the remaining pack of my intentions.

Having successfully seen off all rivals and confirmed my new position, I would then have to enforce my leader's rules on the remaining wolves. A beta has to possess all of the qualities of his/her alphas, so the final decision as to who is elected lies firmly with the pack's leaders.

For their own personal survival and the future survival of the family, this new beta must be chosen with great care. Confirmation of my new position would be secured only when the remainder of my pack decided to back me up when I howled to my rivals.

The following few uncertain nights seemed finally to come down to this one crucial howl. Having first discouraged all rival lone animals and with my alpha beside me, we announced to all the other hopefuls as a new complete pack that the beta position was now filled. The feelings I received from knowing that I had been chosen by my leaders, above all else filled me with a sense of accomplishment never before felt.

I had never done well at school; I was always too busy with my early studies of the animals and the need to be outdoors, to apply myself to the restrictions of a classroom. In a few short breathtaking moments, I had made up for my entire boyhood and teenage failures, not to mention

my final grades! I had graduated with the aid of one of the most demanding sets of teachers in the world!

In all fairness, this had been the part that I had been ably taught by my predecessor. I am entirely convinced that without my beta's help and teaching I certainly would not have been able to achieve my new status. The next stage I would have to learn for myself.

After the pack's night-time activities, the days were used to catch up on vital rest. The warm sun would often put me into a deep sleep (I guess that was still the human coming out in me). I learned quickly that my alpha found this to be totally unacceptable, as he developed his own alarm system for wakening me. He would run over to me, jump in the air and land on me from a height of three-four feet with all four paws. Zac weighs in the region of 110 to115 pounds and by any body's standards that's quite a wake up call!

At first I was puzzled by his actions, assuming them to be hostile. However they were never backed up with aggression, he merely told me to follow him around, whilst he reinforced his scent. At every scent point he stopped and looked back at me, then continued on his way. Once we had completed patrolling our territory, we would then return to our rest.

This went on for several days, until I found myself dreaming that Zac was approaching me. It sounded as if he was wearing clogs! The noise seemed deafening; so much so that it awoke me abruptly and there, just about to launch himself at me, was Zac. He stopped, looked at me and told me it was time for scenting.

Never again have I been caught sleeping. When we rest it is with complete awareness of our environment, much like a mother who can hear her child crying above all other sounds. However, my lesson in identifying my leader's scent was far from over.

When a kill has been made, most people believe that the high ranking animals weald supremacy. In actual fact this is the time when lower ranking animals test their leaders. Under the distraction of food, positions have to be reinforced.

As a beta, my task was to reinforce both my alpha's position and my own, whilst he fed on all the high quality food that maintained his leadership.

Lower ranking animals are called away from the kill to prevent them being distracted by the food. The closer you allow them to the kill, the less effect your discipline will have and accordingly the more you will have to use.

Once a pecking order has been established, my pack rules state that I can return to the kill and eat with the alphas. In some situations, especially in the wild, feeding as quickly as possible is essential. Each wolf may be allocated an area of kill to feed on that is just a few inches wide. Hence the vital importance of maintaining strict order in the pack, something that was to be vividly re-emphasised to me by my own alpha on more than one occasion.

The same misconceptions that have shadowed public opinion about wolves for so long have steadily filtered down to the people who know and care for them most.

It was believed that the safest way to interact with wolves was to dominate them. I feel this could be extremely dangerous. By limiting your understanding to just dominance or submission, a trap that many people fall into, you are limiting both your understanding and also your ability to communicate fully with the animal.

I have always believed that the wolves learn by association, low ranking animals learning from the higher ranking.

Having been taught to always trust in the animals themselves, I know that the wolves are very gentle with those whom they consider to be family.

It was decided to try to infiltrate the pack as a mid to low rank, rather than a high rank. In this way I could climb the strict social structure, learning each rank as the wolves themselves would have to.

In a world where you are constantly tested for the right to hold your position, and in turn you have to test your leaders, this is truly where the battle for survival within the pack begins.

After several months of interaction, I was finally considered by the pack to be worthy of a beta position. This position is high ranking, just below the alphas. It was during this time that I experienced the discipline that can only be given by your alpha.

Part of my duties included control at the kill. Many people believe this is governed by the alphas, but in fact the betas have the main role. This includes calling lower ranking wolves away from the kill to reinforce both your own and your leader's position. This is always better achieved away from the kill, as allowing sub-dominants close to the food at this point, would greatly diminish your authority.

Once a pecking order has been re-established I can then return to the kill, where my pack rules allow me to feed with my alphas, in reward for helping gain access to the carcass by using a tug-of-war motion.

On one particular occasion, the wolves' meal had comprised of one whole carcass and two ducks that had kindly been donated from the local shoot.

Having returned to the kill, my alpha was already eating one of these ducks and had claimed the other by scenting on the bird itself. It was then that I broke one of the most important rules within the wolf pack. I did not identify my alpha's scent on the second duck and moved towards it. In less than a heartbeat I had been pinned to the ground and muzzled.

This involved the wolf clamping his entire mouth over mine. For a moment time seemed to stand still; I questioned almost everything I had ever been taught, should I act like a wolf and submit or simply go with my human instincts and fight back? I think it must have been my Indian teacher's voice, reminding me to always trust in the animals that led to my decision.

I placed my hand on the wolf's chest, a move that should ensure that the grip was released. Having accepted this acknowledgement of his dominance, my leader then showed me that he was every inch the balanced animal I had believed. The grip was instantly released and he was happy just to stand over me, baring his teeth while growling.

At this point my complete submission was communicated by turning my eyes and head to one side, to expose my throat and vulnerable underside. This was totally accepted as he moved away, pausing only briefly to pick up the duck and continue feeding.

This one incident could easily have ended with me being badly hurt, but in fact resulted in not even a mark on the skin. After the event, my leader seemed to sense my uncertainty around him and just as a good father should he came over, rubbed his face against mine and left with an affectionate lick of my nose.

Thankfully he did not check the state of my underwear!

CHAPTER 7

The gift

I was once asked if the work we do with the wolves is unique. My answer to that person is the same answer that I now give to you. Some of the techniques we use are new in many ways but, most of them come from very old ways that have long since been forgotten; passed down from our ancestors who have lived alongside animals such as the wolf, in harmony for thousands of years. Then, people knew how to live as part of nature; never killing more than they could eat, never taking more land than a man could use.

For as long as I can remember I have always shared their respect for the animals and birds that live in our world. As a young boy I would spend many hours looking through books on birds, memorising each one and learning where it was from. For all those that I was unable to remember, I carefully marked the page so I could return to them at a later stage. Soon enough, any bird that was pointed out to me from the book I could name without hesitation.

My earliest impression of wolves was that each night as my bedroom light was put out, I would hide under the prickly old blanket, preferring its rough texture to the outline of the animal that would appear at my window.

Despite knowing that to peep out would scare me beyond belief, I had to take that chance. Slowly peering out from my implement of torture, there in the window I could see the wolf's head, with ears straight up, it was always facing to the left. Quickly, as most boys of that age do, I threw the covers back over my head and there I stayed until the next morning.

As the daylight came my nocturnal visitor disappeared, waiting for the darkness before once more coming to be with me.

Living where I did I was always surrounded by wildlife of many types. Working dogs were heavily used to both help move domestic livestock and to guard remote houses such as ours. The barn used to provide them with warmth and shelter and the straw that was stored inside gave them a comfortable bed.

As a boy I was always a bit of a loner, preferring the company of the dogs to that of other people. Because the dogs were very much left to their own behaviour once they had finished their daily work, they had a very natural rank structure.

Being so young I have no memory of this family bond, or that I had been any part of it, until one morning when I had been woken by a commotion from outside. Bess, the oldest dog, was on his feet, standing with his back legs over my shoulder. His tongue was out and drops of saliva were dripping from his mouth. My movement made him turn his head towards me; blinking, he raised one eyebrow and turned back towards the door.

Settling back down, knowing that Bess would tell me if anyone

came, I began to doze once more just as my name was called from the
back door. Brushing the straw from my trousers and jumper, I hurried
inside. There at the table was one of the farm hands; he had his
handkerchief wrapped around his forearm and tiny spots of blood had
just begun to show through.

Without acknowledging my presence (which in itself was not
unusual) the farmer appeared.

'Can he still use it?'

'Yeah it's just a nip.'

'Wash it out under the tap, I'll fetch the iodine.'

As he left, the farmer's wife guided me to the table. There was a
large chunk of bread waiting, covered in honey.

'He was only protecting the boy,' she called after the farmer. The
muffled reply came from the other room, 'I know, we'll have to keep the
lad from the barn at night in future, any road it's not good for him
sleeping with them dogs.'

My grubby little face was now turning from one voice to the
other, still not understanding what was going on.

'You should know not to go in the barn when that boy is in there anyway.'

'Yeah I know. He din't alf go though, the boy was still asleep, din't bat an eyelid,' replied the farm hand.

All the confusion had been caused by one of the men who worked on the farm trying to pass both the dogs and their sleeping companion - me. He had been after the chain-saw that was kept at the back of the barn when he had sampled the protective instinct of the collie cross.

When faced with what he perceived as danger, Bess had protected his pack with all the loyalty and devotion to family that his wild relatives would have used, probably more. The wolf's natural instinct is to avoid confrontation, whereas our domestic pets have been bred over the years to display slightly more defensive qualities.

Back in the kitchen, the arm had been strapped and the muffled conversation that I could only just hear now turned to my interactions with the dogs. The solution to their problem was decided; rather than risk having the dogs whining throughout the night, or me going to them while the rest of the household slept, they would get a pup that could live in the house.

Whiskey was one of a litter of five pups that belonged to one of our neighbours. In those days your neighbour was considered to be anyone that you could walk to in the space of a day!

With the arrival of daybreak, I sat at the table. The heat from the stove that was boiling water for the farmer's morning tea was too much for the thick jacket I already had on as I waited to leave. The large saucepan was filled with enough water for the labourers who would soon be arriving.

Left on the huge wooden work surface were bread, cheese and a bottle of cold tea. The husky voice of the farmer's wife echoed from the doorway of the large walk-in larder; her face half hidden by the brace of pheasants, three rabbits and one hare that hung from the door. The farmer's wife pointed to the food and drink on the side.

'You can pack that in your bag now,' she told me. Taking the poacher's bag from the hook on the back of the door, I began to collect our lunch.

The farmer asked, 'You ready boy?' I nodded keenly. Gulping down the last of his mug of tea, he kissed the upturned cheek of his wife.

'Won't be long ma,' and with that shortest of exchanges we were gone. As we travelled through the countryside he pointed out all that he had learnt from his father, the rules you should follow regarding the countryside and the creatures that live there.

I used to listen to this man for hours. He fed from the land whilst carefully maintaining the balance of nature so there would always be enough left for tomorrow.

My journey was filled with information, far too much for me to take in. Last year's birds' nests, their young long since flown, were instantly identified. The burrows of rabbits were carefully examined to see if they had been or were currently being worked.

I marvelled at the senses of this man of ageing years. The slightest of movements, the tiniest of sounds, even the different smells that his world provided him with had all contributed to the extraordinary health and fitness that still bore him in good stead.

Reaching our destination, the two gentlemen of about equal age and understanding, greeted each other as only two people who had been friends for their entire life would.

After the brief exchange they both disappeared into the barn.

'Wait there boy. I won't be long' was the last I heard.

Taking a seat on a bale of straw, I did as I was asked. Sometimes these meetings would last several hours so a comfortable position was always a bonus.

Even as one so young my discipline had been taught to me well and if I was told to stay there then I would not dream of moving, regardless of the time scale. My trust in my mentor was such that I knew he would eventually return to where he had left me.

I was suddenly drawn to the creaking of the barn door that lay to my right. The strong breeze that blew through the barn opened the large door about two feet. From inside came the sound of a dog barking.

The figure rushed from the door, moving straight to where I was sitting. From my time with Bess and his pack, the fast approaching animal and his vocal greeting was something I was very familiar with. Usually it was best to let Bess and the remaining dogs greet me. They would tell me what I was allowed to do, growling in a low voice if I displeased them.

I allowed the dog to approach me. As she approached my side I remained still, recognising the low growl as meaning that she was not yet comfortable in my presence. Firstly she familiarised herself with my scent, sniffing my hands, legs, feet and head. Still I remained motionless.

Slowly, after a few seconds, her growling ceased. I turned my hand over so that she could smell my palm. The scent of the cheese that I had packed earlier that morning was still on my hands. She licked at the inside of my hand, her eyes soft as she gazed at my face. Moving one hand, I began to scratch the long fur under her chin.

Bess loved this and I would often see him trying to get the other dogs to do the same thing to him.

Judging from the fact that this animal had now sat down and begun to lean into me so that I could reach other parts of her body, I would say that she too liked this attention.

Looking in the direction of the barn, the animal by my side suddenly gave out another low growl followed by a sharp bark. Jumping to her feet, she raced off in the direction of the barn door from which the two figures now emerged.

From the ensuing panic, I could only assume that the dog that I had been stroking a few seconds ago was not entirely friendly towards visitors. The animal's owner barked out a command.

'Get in that barn!' The dog instantly lowered its body, turned and moved back in my direction. 'Stay still boy,' he commanded, as the dog slunk to my side. She tucked her shaking body close to mine. The only reaction I could think of was to continue with my previous action that had seemed to mellow the dog before. I began to once more scratch the underside of the dog's chin.

'Come an have a look at this.' I looked up; the animal's owner had removed his cap and was now rubbing his head with the same hand. His damp tufts of hair, wet with sweat, standing back up as he tried to flatten them. My still wary mentor had now joined him.

Pausing for a second or two, I heard him say to the dog's owner, 'Ma always said he had some kind of gift with the dogs, I swear he knows what they say.'

Not convinced of their own ability with the animal, who turned out to be the mother of the pups that we were visiting, they decided to shut her away until we left.

Making our way into the barn from which she had first appeared, we moved to an area right at the back that had been secured by bales of straw to prevent the young pups from escaping.

There, curled up in one big ball, were the pups. Varying in colours from black and white to brown and black, there were four girls and one boy. Knowing even at that age from the farmer's teachings that females were renowned for their ability to feed their families, it was one of the bitches that I was after.

The farmer tied a piece of baling twine of about two feet in length around a rabbit's foot that he had brought with him. Making the squeaking sound that would have been made by the rabbit itself, he dangled the string over the bales. Hearing the sound, the pups' ears pricked up, trying to locate the origin of the noise. Seeing the fur dangling within their reach was all the pups needed to spring to their feet. Sure enough, the females were the ones who showed the most interest and after a short while, two of the pups had shown more promise than the remaining two.

'What do ya think boy?'

'That one.'

'You sure?'

'Yeah.'

I had picked Whiskey because I saw so much in her behaviour of what Bess had taught his family. Cradling the tiny pup, I watched as the farmer handed over two large bottles of light ale to the pup's owner; payment for Whiskey.

Shaking hands, I could just about hear the man over the pup's frantic licking, saying, 'the boy was right ya know, she'd be the one I'd 'ave picked.'

With a knowing wink, my mentor acknowledged his statement. The two men bid each other farewell.

'Away ya go boy.' I moved forwards, still clutching Whiskey.

'Thank you sir,' I said. Never forgetting the manners that I had been taught, I was always to address my elders as sir.

'You're welcome boy, look after her.'

Even though the dogs were very much used for work, they were none the less cared for. It was no less important to the pup's owner to find them a good home than it is to dog breeders today.

Over the next few months, Whiskey was taken along whenever they were moving the sheep. Sitting there on my lap, she watched every movement that was made by Bess and the rest of the pack.

After the flock had been safely moved, I took her down to run with the other dogs. Running and playing she was shown how to become a dog by Bess and his family and how to fit in with pack rules. Her remaining teaching was done by myself after she had finished watching them work.

Whiskey was not going to be a herding dog, but she would have to fit in with the resident pack's rules, so she was taken along as part of her training.

The next six months of her life were spent being introduced to fur and feather and the thrill of the chase. Whiskey's breed was Lurcher collie cross, making her incredibly fast over any terrain.

School for the children finished to coincide with the harvest so that we could help gather the corn during the short season.

Whiskey was now two years of age; she had already proven herself a remarkable hunter, feeding the family from the age of fourteen months.

As the low drone of the two huge bright red combine harvesters gathered the crop of corn by the acre, I sat on a nest of straw that I had collected from the offerings the harvester had thrashed out from the back. I waited patiently for any signs of rabbit that might be flushed out by the machines. Whiskey and I watched for any movement.

In a few short hours the tall crop that once covered many acres had been reduced to a small rectangle of approximately two hundred metres by five hundred.

With each round of the combines, the rabbits moved out of the corn towards the hedge. Carefully, Whiskey and I waited for the right animal. I had been taught which animals to take so that future generations could flourish, providing food for others and the creatures that shared our food.

Now into late afternoon, it was time for Whiskey and I to return home, taking enough rabbit to provide supper for the hungry farm hands who would have to work well into the night. I now had to prepare them for the farmer's wife to cook.

Pausing under a tree as I made my way home through the woods, I began to hulk the three rabbits. Giving Whiskey his reward from the proceeds for his part in collecting the meal, I left the remaining unwanted parts of the rabbits for the foxes and any other of nature's residents that rely on the help of animals that make the kill in order for them to feed.

At this time I was unaware of the teachers I was later to meet and their world that so closely matched my early life. Under the wing of my future mentors, I would be told of their honour to the animals that they relied upon for food; how their hunters, out trying to find enough food to feed themselves and their families, would match their skills against some of nature's greatest athletes. Sometimes the animal would give its life to feed a starving family.

Often these people would go hungry. Living as part of nature's Eco-system they too balanced between life and death. After a kill was made, no matter how hungry they were, they would always honour the creature's strength and speed. They would offer their apologies for taking its life before removing the fallen animal's heart; releasing its spirit into the air to be reborn. Sometimes the spirit would enter the soul of a tribal elder, who would take the animal's wisdom to help many of its own kind.

Leaving enough food behind to feed the other animals and birds that shared their lands, the Indians returned to their villages where every part of the animal they called brother would be used. Meat would feed hungry mouths, skin would be used for warmth and bone used to make tools.

Returning home, my first priority was to provide a cool drink for Whiskey. She did not share my love of cold tea, preferring instead to drink from one of the many ponds that we had sat and fished from when she was a pup. Hearing her lapping up the thirst-quenching water, I knew her next move would be to lie down by my feet to rest.

It was time to make a start on the rabbits. A large pan had already been filled with salt water and to one side was a small mountain of freshly prepared vegetables. Making a large stew ensured that regardless of the time the farm workers returned, there would be a hot meal waiting for them that would only require serving; a useful trick for busy lives and one that I often still resort to even now. The only change is that I no longer have to catch and prepare the main ingredient.

As I had made a kill I tried to honour the animals' death in my own way. I, like my future teachers, was taught to use the entire animal that had given its life to feed a hungry and not so wealthy family. All of the meat and bone would go to feed the people and animals, with the dried and cleaned fur making welcome insulation to winter boots during cold weather.

My early years had mostly been spent in the company of dogs and other animals. Unaware of the impact their early teaching would have on me, I continued to prefer their company to that of most people well into my early teens.

Even to this day I often allow myself an inner laugh, when Jan has on more than one occasion, questioned at least one half of my parentage as non human. Now, having read this, it will be hard for me to convince her that her suspicions were ever in doubt!

In my eyes, my mentor had always been a man to look up to, but I never really knew of the thoughts that others had for him. This changed when sadly; this always-active man who I thought would live forever and always be there for me, died.

His funeral service reflected the popularity that came from a man who had always lived his life to the full. I can still remember to this day looking around the huge church at all the faces of those who knew him.

Sitting at the back was a small family consisting of a young man and woman in their mid-late thirties with what I assumed were their two children. I did not recognise them as friends of the family but thought little of their presence.

After the service, this man stopped me and offered his condolences. He apologised for not returning sooner but he and his family had moved away when he was very young. As we talked, he told that as a small boy he, his mum and dad and his brothers and sisters were very poor. His mother used to make him follow the bread cart that delivered the bread to the more wealthy families, waiting for any pieces that might be left at the end of the day or that might be dropped in the street and discarded. He finished his story by telling me that the farmer had seen him as a boy with his little sister, holding her hand as they both followed the chance for some food.

'Wait here boy and look after your sister,' he said. He then went to the back of the cart and selected two large loaves of bread. He gave one each to the children and told them to run home with them as fast as they could, then he paid for them.

The young boy grew to a man along with his brothers and sisters and now he had children of his own, but he had never forgotten the act of kindness that fed him and his family. He had returned many years later, travelling from one end of the country to the other, to thank the man who had made such a lasting impression on a very small boy and his sister. It now seems to me that making lasting impressions on the people who knew him was a natural part of his life.

As for me, I will never forget the man who has taught me so much.

Shortly after the death of my mentor, the farm no longer functioned as a place of work. The farm hands who had been there from when they too were still schoolboys, moved to new employment.

As for the farmer's wife, she never really seemed to come to terms with her husband's death. They had married shortly after leaving school and he had always been with her throughout every day of their lives. It seemed to me that she simply could not stand the thought of being without him. A few short months after his death she too (one night whilst sleeping) returned once more to the side of the man she had loved for so long.

C H A P T E R 8

A new beginning

Now, as a young man, everything that I had held onto so closely was gone. All that now remained was the pup that both the farmer and me had travelled many miles to collect so many years ago.

Trying to make sense of the blow that life had now dealt me, I walked the same path that we used when we went to collect Whiskey. Now an old dog, she struggled to keep the faithful position by my side, that once she held so impatiently.

Together we found a fallen tree that made a comfortable place to rest. Watching her sitting there looking up at me, licking around her muzzle that now contained many grey whiskers and seeing the slow gentle way she moved to lay down by my side, I realised that my last remaining companion was also getting old.

I reached into the bag that I always carried which contained mine and Whisky's lunch, I took out the bread and cheese and offered some to her. As she had always done, she carefully took the food from my hand.

Where I had once struggled to keep her with me, she now seemed to welcome the rest that was provided. Even the constant movement of the animals and birds in the surrounding countryside no longer made any impression on her. She had now become as dependent on me for her food as I had been on her all those years ago.

For many years now I had closely followed the lives of the fox families that lived close by and where previously I had to leave Whiskey behind, she now offered no threat to them. We both spent many days and nights just sitting and watching them grow.

Often the long nights out in the cold and sometimes wet weather (when the foxes are most active) proved to be too much for Whiskey. As I packed my gear and dressed for the cold night ahead, I would look down to where she had always slept.

Even as a pup her place had always been with me, lying under the bed with just her muzzle showing. She had been my constant companion but now, as I looked at her soft eyes, asking whether she wanted to join me, she would raise one eyebrow and look up at me. Our night-time strolls that she had once so looked forward to, now proved to be beyond her.

I would bend down and give her a familiar scratch under her chin and tell her that it was all right, I could manage without her help just this once. From beneath the bed came the familiar thumping sound that meant her tail was wagging with approval, firstly at the prospect of staying warm and dry but, I think most of all, the fact that I could only manage without her help this one time.

Over the next few weeks, Whiskey and I bid farewell to the home where we had both grown up. If I were to continue the work I had come to love so much, I would have to take other part-time employment so that we would be able to live.

Both of us had been brought up to be survivors and the lessons we had learnt would make us strong enough to cope with whatever life could throw our way. The ever-increasing building work that seemed to be growing overnight around us provided most of our income, whilst the part time game-keeping offered us something of the old life we used to know.

The next few years were to prove to be a difficult adjustment from the life we once knew. Whiskey's health began to fade and finally, having spent two days and nights desperately trying to get her to feed, her head resting in my lap, she slipped away.

We had spent the last hours of her life very much as we had begun them on the day she was collected, with her head resting on me as I scratched her under the chin. Sitting there in the dark, still stroking her, I said my final good-bye to all the family who had made my childhood such an education and a wonder. Without them, the life that I had come to know no longer held the same meanings.

The next morning, just after sunrise, I carried Whiskey to the place where she was to finally rest, the same place where she once loved to run and play as we walked.

With the tears of a lifetime of memories still running down my face, I picked up the bag that now contained my belongings and began to turn and face an uncertain future.

Without any formal training and very little schooling, I began to study and research my first Canids. It had taken me a long time and many careers, that had seen me labouring and even doing a brief spell in the armed forces, before I had finally come to realise where my future lay. I had come full circle to once more be with the animals that I had begun with all those years ago.

The only things that were absent were the companions that used to be at my side. Staring up at the night sky and the millions of stars that filled it, the memories of old and trusted friends and the many lessons they taught me still remained with me. I wonder if they had any say in my decision to return?

My first concern was for the future of the foxes. Like most Canids, they too had suffered from the effects of living with a bad reputation. Their enthusiasm for raiding hen houses and making off with one bird, having killed all but a very few of the remainder had put them, in the eyes of the people of the countryside, on Britain's most wanted list. If seen in and around domestic livestock or fowl, the fox would be shot at without hesitation.

But, why does this once shy and retiring animal now come to our farms, towns and cities for its food where once it was never seen? The answer that I came up with all those years ago whilst studying them, was that we are now the only remaining large predator from whom the fox can scavenge. Equally, all but a handful of the natural prey animals of the fox have also moved to our farms and towns, having been forced to give more of their wild countryside to an ever expanding human society. We offer their best chance of survival.

In the early days of my life, we still had the chance to live alongside our fellow creatures and many of the farmers were happy to do just that. With their livestock and poultry safely secured from the foxes' seemingly supernatural ability to break into, climb over and dig under even the most challenging of constructions. At that time the farmers began to see the fox for the good that it did in checking numbers of its natural prey, such as rats and mice, along with crop-destroying insects that if left to breed as they pleased would in fact reach uncontrollable numbers.

I finally settled, close to a small village in the heart of the country. The small, solitary, ivy-cloaked cottage that I rented was the first place I had called home for many years. It proved to be an ideal setting to be close to the creatures I now worked with.

Early one evening there was a faint knock on the door of the cottage. I received very few visitors and the ones who did call would only do so by prior arrangement, due to the nature of my work and their slim chances of finding me at home.

As I opened the door, I could hear the voice of a woman seemingly talking to herself or, as I thought at the time, rehearsing what she was going to say. The figure before me was an elderly lady, small in stature with a good head of white hair. She wore a long dark trench coat that she held together with her hands.

After exchanging greetings she told me that a gentleman in the village, who thought I might be able to help her, had given her my name. I invited her inside and asked her how I could help.

'Well, it's this.' Her accent was unmistakably local. From where she sat opposite me, she reached inside her coat and took out a young fox kit, handing it to me.

She said, 'It wandered into the barn two days ago and we fed it.' The fox kit was a dog of only a few weeks old, too young to be roaming.

The tiny animal was probably orphaned as result of its parents being killed. This often happens on our roads that alone take enough foxes each year to control their numbers. This would have accounted for the kit's lack of body fat, otherwise he seemed to be in good health.

The lady could not tell me where the young fox had lived and she did not know of any others in her area. I asked her if the animal had been exposed to many people, to which she replied that there was only her and her son who had been anywhere near the fox.

She asked me what I would do with the animal and I told her that I would attempt to re-release it back into the wild as soon as it was old enough. The woman thanked me for my help, wished me luck and bid me farewell.

I made my way to the barn and set up an enclosure for the fox. Using one of the large pipes that had been used for drainage, I made him a den and darkened the area, attempting to recreate his natural environment.

Fetching him from the house, I placed him in the straw-based bed that would be his home for the next few weeks. In the wild, young foxes, especially dog foxes, can be anything up two hundred and fifty kilometres from their place of birth. If they find their own territory, they will lay among the thick brush throughout the winter until spring, when they will seek a mate and breed that year.

Until the fox kit had learnt how to hunt, where to find his food and how to eat it, I would have to take on the role of one of his parents. The next few weeks were spent dividing my time between studying and teaching Barney (as I named him) his natural role as a hunter.

Fortunately, the many cats living close by caught small animals such as rats, mice and rabbits and this provided Barney with a good supply of his natural food. I avoided feeding him lamb or chicken based foods, for fear of introducing him to a liking for food that would be likely to cause him problems in later life.

This was only a theory that I had at that time. I had witnessed interesting behaviour from vixens I had studied, bringing stillborn lambs or even afterbirth that had been left, to their kits. The effect that this early type of food had on the young foxes as they reached adulthood made me very careful about Barney's feeding.

He soon became aware that every time I came into him I had brought him food. He would wag his tail, grin, and pant fast and loud to greet me. Moving the partially skinned food around in front of him, I slowly introduced him to fur, steadily increasing it as he grew more in confidence.

He was also made to defend his food once he had it. I adopted the same form of correction his mother would have used, a fast cacking sound whilst opening the mouth wide. He now used this communication to tell me that this was his meal.

The games I played with him hid an important message, the one of survival. Not only was I his surrogate parent but I had also taken on the role of his littermates.

I had seen this behaviour from vixens who only produced one cub or whose other kits had died, leaving just one. In these situations a vixen would seem to take on both roles, that of parent and sibling, underlining the importance of the education the young foxes gain from the time with their brothers and sisters.

Competition among siblings is very strong, never more so than when food is present, a lesson I learned all too well when I tried to take Barney's food from him. He would place his front paws on my shoulders or bite the back of my neck with a disciplining shake to the scruff if more intensity was needed.

With his strong stand-off attitude to the smell of other people and his instinctive fear of anything that was not familiar, Barney would soon be ready for release.

Over the next few nights I took Barney to the area where he would be finally released. I spent all night encouraging him to listen to the many sounds, among them those of his own kind.

In the wild my observations had told me that foxes rarely disperse at random, they seem to stand more chance of survival if allowed to pick their way through neighbouring territories avoiding injury, enabling them to find and then occupy their own territory in the best of health.

For Barney to be able to do this I had to allow him to hear the sounds that would guide him to his own stretch of land. The nights that I had spent out with Barney and the fact that he now showed me signs of territorial possession whilst there, told me it was time for him to make his own way in life.

As I took him to the release area, I recapped on his teaching. I had covered all the lessons that I knew from watching many wild foxes with their young, plus one other that I felt he may need one day, a fear of dogs and the ability to detect them at the earliest moment. As I released him I had no way of knowing whether or not my training would aid him throughout his life.

With one dash he made his way towards the trees, stopping momentarily at the edge of the wood to turn his head back towards me once and then he was gone.

The next few years as I travelled to new areas looking for any signs of dispersal among the family of fox that I was studying, I would sometimes catch sight of the wild fox who I had once named Barney, just as nature had intended him to be, running free.

It was those early years that helped shape my life, my only ambition was to work alongside the animals I had come to know and trust. Now, once more returning to my wolf family, it was those early teachings that guided me through my work. The help of the animals through my early years remains my drive to protect creatures and the world they live in. My mentor once told me to use the gift that I had been given wisely. I hope, with their help, I have done so.

CHAPTER 9

A new generation

We were now into late summer. The autumn leaves had already begun to cover the ground and the wolves were beginning to acquire their thick winter coats that would offer them protection throughout the long winter months.

Their hackles, (the teardrop shaped hair running down the back, that is so important in wolf communication and behaviour) would reach almost three to three and half inches in length throughout the summer. It would then keep steadily growing to five and a half inches during winter,

making the wolves look increasingly impressive as the build up to the breeding season grew ever nearer, clearly underlining the importance of coat patterns among the wolves. These same patterns were to have an even greater impact on our research.

At this time of the year all thoughts turn to the next generation of wolves and which adults will have earned the rights as alphas to pass on their genes. I have regularly witnessed this type of behaviour with many different wolves. One Crop constantly tested Fang around breeding season. Often using play to instigate, he would constantly place his paws across the back of or even actually mount his leader during courtship with Zeva, making it as difficult as possible for them to mate!

Whenever Fang and Zeva came together One Crop was with them, subtly placing his own body between those of his leaders. Fang's reaction to all this was extremely well balanced, as you would come to expect from one who has led his pack for many years. He seemed to almost tolerate the young wolf's presence, seeing it perhaps as a means to an end.

In all wolf packs the possibility of passing on genes creates a natural high tension among them. As with One Crop and Fang, Reuben used the same testing on Zac but the leader, whilst still maintaining the wolf's balance, simply increased the frequency of reinforcing his own leadership to cover the time of high tension caused by the female's season.

Never did I witness either of them increase the severity of their authority; a view that was clearly shared by the lower ranking wolves the second danger threatened them. Like me, they all knew instantly who to run to.

The significance of this type of balanced control was brought home to me some years ago when I was asked by a friend of Jan's to look at their domestic dog. He had been re-homed with them and was now showing signs of what they described as aggression towards them and other dogs.

The animal, far from showing a high level of dominance and aggression did in fact display a lack of trust in its new owners. The animal would instantly adopt a sphinx-like posture whenever someone approached him, protecting his vulnerable underside. The showing of the underside will only be given when complete trust has been gained.

Long ago when I first entered the Dartmoor pack I was accepted by most of the family members but there was one wolf that stayed away from the remaining group, Sheba. Sheba was a low ranking female and for a wolf showed very little trust in any member of the pack, especially me. She preferred to stay below ground during the day in a den of her own making, only venturing out under the cover of darkness. We would instantly know when she was above ground. Her scent was laced with the smell of clay from spending so much time in her den.

I spent many hours resting beside the wolves in my familiar posture that had been taught to me by my leader; head resting on my crossed arms, raising my nose just enough from the ground to pick off any new scent. The scents were brought to us on the faint breeze that used to blow in from the moors during the long summer months.

It was here that I suddenly became very aware of just how much I had become like those around me. The many years spent living with my adopted families had left nothing to chance, even down to the way my head was now tilted slightly to one side mirroring the others, listening to Sheba's distinctive footsteps as she moved around the pack. Sheba used to flick her feet forwards. Always staying low to the ground she walked on very light feet, this was far removed from the sure-footed trot of the alphas.

Slowly over the years the bond between Zac, Sheba and myself has steadily grown. She now allows me to sniff and rub along her back whilst she lowers herself to my rank. As for turning her underside to me, she offers more and more each day.

From underground nocturnal ghost, to valuable pack member, she has come so far in such a short time. I personally feel that her trust in me will soon be complete.

To return to the problems of the domestic dog, patience and a gaining of the animal's trust (in my opinion) were the only techniques required but to gain this trust needs a little understanding.

Whenever a wolf displays this type of body posture the animal is barely even touched by the rest of the pack. The dominant animal is usually satisfied to merely stand over the subservient. If any touch is used at all it will be an affectionate lick to accept the respect that has just been offered.

Turning the dog over when it was a pup would have taught the animal the correct response to that rank. Should that rank change hands (or paws, in this case) in the eyes of the dog, then it will show the correct response to the new rank holder.

As with any alpha within a wolf pack it is not the animal that has the respect, but the rank it holds. Take away that rank and the animal no longer has the respect of submissive wolves. More importantly the young animal should have been taught the importance of trust.

The previous owner had neglected the balance that is so important to wolves and their descendants. This case was by no means cruelty or neglect; the owner had simply paid the price for wanting his dog to have a high level of obedience.

As part of a pack of wolves you do not have the luxury of sit, down, heel, and stay commands. We have to rely on a bond that is formed from the very first time the alpha female allows us to see her pups. These precious moments when the young wolves first meet their pack mates bond them to us, in most cases for life.

Under the strict guidance of the alpha female we are shown how to teach the young wolves, guiding them to adulthood using methods the wolves have used for hundreds of years. If the pack is to survive we must rely on these young animals in the not too distant future, when they will be taught through patient tuition and association to take their rightful place within the family.

Over the next few weeks I spent many hours with the dog and its owners, teaching the owners the correct way to approach their dog, using subtle body language along with the right facial expressions.

A higher ranking animal moving towards a subservient can be a fairly tense situation for the lower rank. The correct exchange of communication between the two of them as the dominant animal approaches is all that is usually required to calm the situation.

I can still see to this day, the look on their faces as I began to demonstrate the correct movement by a high ranking wolf and the fact that the wrong facial expressions will only serve to confuse the animal, making it even less trustworthy.

I looked at Jan and just like the wolves, we too in this instance did not need to say a word. I rose to my feet slowly; pausing only briefly to look back at the rest of the family that had now been joined at the table by Jan. That was my cue. I stretched, yawned and slowly began to move down the long corridor to the kitchen where the dog was lying. My stride was sure and true like that of my alphas, my body posture full of self confidence, my head held slightly low, facing in the direction of the dog. Only my eyes now told the animal that I meant him no harm, with soft expression and eyes turned slightly to one side, I only met his gaze long enough for him to see me blink and then look away.

At this stage I had no idea what the dog knew of wolf communication or if the dog itself would respond. Early signs were good; the dog mimicked my own communication and then just as nature intended, when I had reached the side of the animal, being the more dominant of the two, I moved in above the dog.

I began randomly sniffing him in the same way I had with the wolves on many occasions before. Firstly lifting his paw, he displayed his light throat and chest, his head completely over to one side. I tried to remember the wolves' system, carefully going through everything they had ever taught me and then I once again saw the extended paw.

All those exchanges between my pack mates and myself now came to me with great clarity. My mind raced, 'Of course - the sweat gland under the inside leg - this access would give another animal all the information it would require to communicate and get the history from a lower rank'.

I moved down the dog's body towards the abdomen, slowly encouraging it to turn on its side, offering me complete trust. After a brief exchange of mutual sniffing we parted and the dog settled back down to rest.

Contemplating whether the approach of the animal and our interaction had been correct, I gazed upwards, instantly catching the table full of open mouths belonging to those who had just witnessed what had happened and Jan's voice telling them that Shaun obviously knows wolves'/dogs' body postures. It did not appear to be having much impression on them, they were still trying to come to terms with what they had just seen, man and dog communicating, using one universal language.

The next few weeks saw a remarkable change in the dog's

owners' understanding of their animal. Having seen firsthand the intricate language exchanged between our fellow creatures and ourselves. Just a small amount of understanding was all it took to convince them to learn the dog's language. To this day, both dog and family live with one language and in complete harmony.

To return to the wolves, Zeva's role as the Alpha female begins long before she thinks about falling pregnant. She (like Fang the alpha male) must re-assert her dominance.

With just over four and a half months to go until she produces her pups, Zeva should have already chosen the young wolves' nanny. The candidate can be either male or female, with the wolf being chosen because of their ability to care for and educate the young, rather than for their gender.

From the back of the Rover the team congratulated me. I had managed to miss one of the many potholes that had covered them in equipment during our journey to the small copse that would provide me with my home for the next week or so.

As I cleared a site for the ground sheet of the tent, I managed to find some old pellets that the owls had regurgitated. From the remains it looked as if their diet consisted mainly of small rodents that still managed to thrive in the untouched countryside that surrounded the small group of trees.

Looking up at the old hollow tree I just couldn't help but feel that if only it could talk, what a tale those weary old branches could tell. Maybe over the next few days and nights it would share some of its secrets with me.

All of the equipment was now unloaded and the tent was up. The old hollow tree's large trunk provided me with ideal shelter from the wind and a good observation point from which I could monitor the wolves. I bade my farewell to Jan and the rest of the team and settled down under the tree.

By now it was late afternoon. The wolves were already becoming active and small amounts of play had broken out among pack members. Their games were very familiar to me; I had come to know them all during my time with the wolves. A student once asked me how such games began. It's more a question of when do such games begin.

The games I used to play with the wolves were done to practice our hunting techniques. Defending yourself against a challenge either from within or outside of the pack, play also provides lower ranking animals with the opportunity to test the more dominant without the risk of injury. As you can imagine, the wolves soon picked me off with their speed so I tried to avoid too much open space, using the trees to keep them turning.

These chasing games would often finish with a quick bout of wrestling. Having practised catching imaginary prey using fellow pack members, they now practised killing it, targeting areas such as flanks and neck.

As with most things that happened within the wolf pack, Zac as alpha, usually began our games, stalking me from a distance. My reaction would be to play bow, placing myself in a position of readiness from which I could defend. If I was happy for us to play, my bow would move from one side to the other telling my alpha that I was comfortable with the level of play. If things got too intense then I would simply just remain in the play bow, motionless, the front half of my body low and the top half high, to tell my leader that I was uneasy with the game and things needed to calm down before we continued.

As I sat resting against the old hollow tree I began to cast my mind back to the very first time Zac, my alpha, caught me during a game of hare and hounds. Early morn; the sun had begun to dapple the thin layer of cloud that had brought us a refreshing shower of rain, washing away the sleep from our eyes after a long restful night and a welcome break from the many biting insects that accompany the summer sun.

Zac was stretching off the night's lack of activities before making his way towards my resting-place. His rigid posture froze every time I raised my head. Once again he edged forwards, I raised only my eyes this time, catching him in mid movement.

He froze again but, by this time I was already on my feet and stretching after a long yawn to announce my intentions; I began to move into the ready bow.

In the few seconds it took him to get to me (covering maybe 50 metres in distance) I had managed to bounce at least five to six times from one side to the other, indicating to Zac my intention to continue. As he approached me, I moved quickly to the side out of his way (pack rules must still be respected). As he turned I was already back in the ready bow. After interlocking briefly, trying to grab at each others scruffs, I broke free from his grasp and set off across the small area of open ground trying to make the tree line before Zac managed to catch me.

The heavy shower of rain had left the ground with a very slippery surface and just before getting to full speed one quick turn to the right was all it took and I was down. Luckily the combination of the slippery ground and my turn had caught Zac off-guard. As I fell, I looked up only to see Zac disappearing over my right shoulder.

Quickly scrambling to my feet I once more made for the tree line. This time I had gone but a few feet when I felt Zac's teeth around the bottom of my calf. Instinctively I turned and growled at my leader, knowing I was not breaking any pack rules by doing so. Zac (like all alphas) was balanced and knew what he could expect from such games, he released me and set off in the direction of the trees.

In the open I would not stand a chance, but among the trees his twisting and turning allowed me to catch him and grab his flank. My leader turned towards me, offering me the same treatment that I had just given him. The difference is that I did not let go.

Sometimes during these games the wolves would hang on to the leg taking it a bit further, testing the defensive skills of a dominant animal. This was my test to my leader. Zac, however, had seen it all before and with one grasp held me by the back of the neck, a price I now paid for having my head too low, making it easy for him to grab me. My only defence was to keep low, pulling one of his front feet. He would risk losing his balance if he continued with the hold so the grip was released.

After reinforcing our bonds, both Zac and I returned to our resting-places totally unhurt; the only difference in our condition was the fact that he was a lot less out of breath than myself!

There's something magical about running with a pack of wolves as day breaks through the trees. The cold of the rain meets the warmth of the day, creating a thin layer of mist over the ground from which you can smell and hear everything from several metres away.

From the nearby farmer's dogs' first walk of the day, to the smell of the diesel engines of the trains that travelled by, they all become part of your world. Knowing these sounds and smells makes it easy to detect ones that should not be there.

Having successfully gained the leadership, Zeva now had to defend it under the most extreme circumstances. We wondered if her youth would cause her a problem. Daisy's wealth of experience as a beta, under Macha's leadership, would be a test for any wolf, especially one so young and inexperienced.

Normally, among healthy wolves the two deciding factors that divide rival pack members are size and more importantly experience. In Zeva's case she had youth and strength on her side but she also gave away a good deal of experience to Daisy.

Over the next few days, from my observation point, I was witnessing an increase in the wolves' games amongst a tiny group of animals: Fang, Zeva and Daisy. Slightly away from the others, these three wolves would now form the basis of the pups' upbringing.

Zeva had put her play among the adults to good use. Over the last few days she had used the wolves' own selection process to choose the pups' nanny.

With each day passing a different adult would be dropped from her programme, sometimes more than one, leaving just one remaining adult, Daisy. She had come full circle to once more show the patience and balance needed to guide the next generation of wolves.

Seeing her resting there with her two leaders made me feel like a father that had just finished watching his daughter's first school play. I had proudly and nervously gone through every line, willing her not to forget them and was now standing there applauding her faultless performance. She had proven to me all that I believed to be true of the wolves.

The admiration that my teachers have for these animals is totally justified. Seeing them as they really are, mankind could find that the wolves would teach us far more than they would ever take from us.

As for our fears of Zeva's leadership qualities, they had turned out to be totally unjustified. Zeva had come a long way, she had proven herself beyond any doubt to be a true alpha, even wise old Daisy with all her years of experience had failed to ruffle her, she was now ready to mother the future of the pack.

In the days that followed, Zeva prepared her pack for the arrival of her young. Carefully, she divided her time between Fang, Daisy and the remaining adults.

Zeva's first concern was to make Fang aware of her scent. She had not yet come into season but would already be giving off a slightly different odour. Fang needed to be familiar with her scent so he would be able to detect the slightest of changes that would tell him she was in season.

Many times throughout the day she would rise from her resting position and after stretching would go to Fang. Sometimes Fang would get to his feet as she approached him. Knowing the importance of the pair bond between them he was usually ready to court Zeva but, more importantly, his concern would lay with the possibility of another male mating with her if he did not.

She moved straight to his muzzle, confident, her head held high and her tail vertical, preventing him from moving off by placing her body in front of him. After they had greeted one another, she would turn and move off but not before giving Fang full access to her scent.

In the few minutes that followed, Zeva, Fang and Daisy fully indulged in the play that would bond them together during the pups upbringing; running, chasing, rolling, scenting. From the outside world it all looks like one big game but their play is balanced and carefully engineered to both test and bond each pack member to ensure the strongest, healthiest genes are passed to the next generation of wolves.

January brought an increase in the hours of daylight and with it Zeva's season. For the next few weeks she would become the centre of attention among the wolves. Behaviour between the two genders would now reach an all time high.

For Zeva, suppression of lower ranking females, preventing them from falling pregnant was just one of the many duties she must perform during her season.

As for Fang, he now faced probably the most important test of his leadership so far, as the alpha male. Time was definitely not on his side. Now, at the age of fifteen, Fang would have to once more prove that he still possessed the strength and good health required to father Zeva's pups; under the constant attention of younger adults just waiting for the first slip that would allow them to pass on their own genes.

During the next few weeks we saw an all time high in the amount of play that took place among the wolves. They had all come through an amazing year and the level of play among them just goes to prove its significance in bonding the wolves together at such an important time.

Zeva and Fang had successfully paired with one another; all that now remained was for me to witness a successful mating between the two of them. The actual copulation between wolves tends to be a very private affair and the last three nights of Zeva's receptive period had not yet resulted in visual confirmation.

I was now in my third week in the copse. Old Hollow, as I had now come to call the hollow tree and I had become very good friends. It had shared with me the secrets of the animals and birds that lived in and around the small group of trees and had even invited them to visit with me as I watched the wolves. In return I had shared all the information I had gained over the last few weeks, along with a large amount of my food, with its local residents.

The green light of the night vision goggles turned night into day as I scanned the clearing before me in search of the wolves. Just inside the tree-line they still remained motionless in their own individual scrapes.

Sitting back down I decided to allow myself the luxury of a phone call to Jan, hoping to catch the kids before they went to bed. I briefly gave Jan an update on the situation, after which she told me that the children were already asleep. They had been to Granny and Granddad's where the combination of plenty of food and the excitement of a day's activities had left them needing an early bed.

Jan told me not to worry; she had constantly shown them pictures of me explaining that this was their father and that one-day he would return! I thanked her for her kind gesture before I realised that it was not meant as an act of kindness but an indication as to the length of time I had been away. Unfortunately, a combination of lack of sleep and still having one ear trained on the wolves put me on a completely different level from that of Jan's quick-witted sense of humour.

Our conversation was suddenly cut very short. The wolves had begun to howl. Maybe they were testing to see how close neighbouring packs were before taking the decision to mate. I switched on the night vision goggles and watched the area of open ground in front of me where I had hoped the wolves would be. There was no sign of them. Still hidden by the trees, only their sound could be heard piercing the night air.

I sat motionless as the last calls now faded. I replied to their inquiry, making sure the volume of the tape was turned low to give the impression that the pack's location was at the far side of their territory. If the wolves had heard no reply they would have continued to call until they located their rivals, suspending their mating until they gained the necessary information. My calls should give them all they needed to begin copulation.

For almost an hour, I watched to see if the wolves would move into the clearing. I knew they were close because of the amount of noise they were making, clearly indicating that wherever they were, the wolves were preparing to mate.

I felt deep down that the silence that followed and now filled the air hid the wolves mating and then, without warning, they suddenly appeared. Both Zeva and Fang were now right in the centre of the clearing. I willed them to stay there as they began their mating. Zeva stood with her rump towards me and slightly on an angle, facing to the right. Fang had already begun to move in behind her. As he approached she lifted her tail slightly and moved it to one side, indicating her readiness to mate. Fang lowered his head and began to lick at Zeva's vulva.

This type of behaviour is all part of the build up to the pair mating, the close attention seeming to increase the male's arousal. Zeva lowered the front half of her body to accept Fang. After mounting her and ejaculating he strode over her so that the pair were now standing locked together facing in different directions, 'tied'.

Despite popular belief 'tying' of the pair is not always required to insure a fertile mating, however if the situation changes and the pair are threatened they can actually run very well from this position.

I sat beneath Old Hollow, reflecting on how far the pack had come, as their howls once more echoed through the great forest. This one night symbolised that a new generation of wolves had been conceived.

CHAPTER 10

The pups

The late arrival of the pups had caused everyone a great deal of worry. Had Zeva lost her young during the early stages of term and was she now displaying the phantom pregnancy, which is very common among wolves? Or was she simply displaying another wolf trait that science has suspected for so long but, as yet very little information is known about, that of actually withholding the birth of their young to coincide with that of their natural quarry.

Due to an outbreak of foot and mouth at this time only essential staff were being allowed access to the animals, so we had to rely on information passed to us by the keepers and staff.

Trying to take full advantage of the situation, we began to look into the possibility that a late birth could in fact be taking place. The rainfall over the last month had reached record amounts but, would this be enough to delay the arrival of the wolves' natural quarry that they would so heavily rely on in the wild at this time of year?

Also these were captive animals. We had made their environment as natural as possible but would this and hundreds of years of instinct be enough to make them behave as their wild brothers? All the information we received back pointed to the fact that the young of the wolves' natural quarry were indeed late.

We began to search through our records to when the keepers and ourselves had witnessed the first mating of Zeva taking place. To actually try to gain the exact date of conception would be almost impossible and would place the wolf under a great deal of pressure.

We have to assume that the first day the alpha female becomes receptive and mates, she could have conceived. As she is receptive for four to six days it is also possible that she may not conceive until the final day. All this information made our pups between one and two weeks overdue, along with those of many other captive packs in parks throughout the UK.

Finally the phone call that we had all waited for came. Zeva had given birth to three tiny pups. Weighing only one pound each, the pups were reported to be suckling and both mum and young were doing well.

The conversation between the wolves' keeper and myself was one of relief and joy. It was also very brief. Not knowing yet of the information we had collected, he apologised for not being able to talk longer as over the last two to three days they had become very busy. All the deer had begun to give birth to their young. Nearly two weeks overdue, Zeva had timed the birth of her young to coincide exactly with that of the deer. Coincidence? Knowing the wolves I very much doubt it.

The next three weeks were a very frustrating time for me and the rest of the team. Unable to visit the wolves because of the foot and mouth outbreak, we began to tackle the mountain of paper work that had built up over the past few busy months. This included notes that I had made on the effects of wolves, actively communicating with one another, on neighbouring wildlife and in particular those that would be naturally preyed upon by the wolves.

Having an active pack of wolves close to a herd of deer or any other of the wolf's quarry is perfectly natural in the wild but this was captivity. Here of course, the animals do not have the luxury of flight that their wild relatives could exercise. Great care must be taken to ensure no undue stress is caused by the interaction between the wolves and ourselves.

All the results however turned out to be entirely positive. After the mating season, the deer took to the cover to give birth, hiding their young from predators as opposed to using the open ground that they had favoured before. They also began herding together during the cold winter months, reducing the number of old animals that would normally fall foul to the severe weather.

In the wild I suspect that all these tiny aspects play a vital role in the survival of both predator and prey. In nature, many of the prey animals that the wolves feed upon are more than capable of defending one calf against the wolves. Where they seem to struggle is with the old and sick animals. Finding it near impossible to keep with the herd when the wolves run them, they quickly fall victim to the pack.

Do the herds have some hidden agenda for prolonging the life of these old animals when they hear the wolves howl? Or is it merely instinct that makes them herd together?

The other factor that seems to come up time and again is the herds' ability to produce twins whenever wolves are close to them.

Another important issue when working close to civilisation is the effect the wolves might have on domestic livestock. Keeping in touch with farmers and ranchers is very important. I began passing time with the local shepherds that run their sheep close to the parks. Always happy to discuss their livestock, they are a good source of information on the effects the wolves are having on any on their animals.

One spring, Jan and I were chatting to one of the local shepherds, asking him how this year's young were doing. He was unaware of what we did, merely knowing that we worked at the park with the wolves. I asked him whether over the last four years there had been any change in his flock? After thinking long and hard, he replied that the only real significant change among the sheep was an abnormal amount of twins that had been born during this time.

Over the next few weeks we received regular updates on the wolves. They were growing well on their mother's rich milk and there was an air of excitement now surrounding the adults.

Only one scare shadowed an otherwise perfect first few weeks. Zeva had given birth in the den and although it offered the ideal conditions for her to raise her pups in the most natural environment, our good old British weather can cause a big problem to young helpless wolves. The den that can easily flood with the amount of rain we receive.

One evening, keepers listened to the torrential rain that fell throughout the night, feeling helpless and very concerned for the new pups' welfare. Roads quickly turned into rivers, as the already soaked ground could take no more water. Fearing the worst, the devastation caused by the rain was all too evident en route to the wolves the next morning. The waterlogged scene did nothing to encourage any optimism in the already concerned staff.

There were no signs of the pups in the den. All the keepers' worst fears now looked like becoming a reality. Desperate to be proven wrong they decided to check the house, a man-made shelter that had been built for the wolves which had, in the past, been used to raise their pups. There in the warm fresh straw lay three tiny bundles of fur, protected by their mother as she suckled them.

Once more, against all that nature could throw at them, the wolves had come through it all. During the night Zeva and the rest of the adults, knowing that the den would soon become flooded, had moved the young pups several hundred metres by carrying them in their mouths to the safety of the house. This amazing demonstration of pack loyalty once again places the wolves on an equal footing with our own family bonds.

The next week brought both changes in the weather and an increase in the number of times the young wolves were seen out with the adults. Excited members of staff boasted of seeing the pups whilst checking on the wolves, others told of their disappointment at not yet being lucky enough to be there when the young wolves were out.

With the foot and mouth restrictions now lifted, we were able to visit the pups for ourselves. Upon arriving I called in at the office. Everyone was very pleased with the new arrivals and for several minutes conversation centred around them. The only reason we stopped talking was that as I looked across at Jan her face reflected my own inner feelings, we must go and see the pups for ourselves. We were told by keepers not to be disappointed if the young wolves did not appear. I simply winked at them and Jan and said, 'Don't worry we won't be'.

We were told where the pups were last seen, but it was not the same place that the wolves now told me they were. Moving around to where the adults were positioned I saw Daisy slightly away from the group. She lay exactly as she had so many times before whilst guarding Macha's pups. This was where we would find the young wolves, carefully hidden from view by the tree roots just below the surface.

I have slowly got used to the expressions on people's faces telling me they question my sanity. Only Jan's facial expression now told me that she trusted in something she had seen time and again. I believed that the pups were close by and from the smile on my face she also knew it would not be long before they showed themselves.

As Zeva moved towards the den, pausing momentarily to greet Daisy, I shuffled in my seat. Daisy moved to a position from which she could defend and a high pitched whimper now filled the air, as Zeva called her pups to suckle. In a matter of seconds one, then two and finally three tiny figures appeared at their mother's side, greedily feeding as she stood over them.

From where we were I could finally manage to make out that the three pups were two boys and one girl. After feeding, they gently bonded with their mother and Daisy until the few minutes' activity tired the pups sufficiently for them to return to their resting place under the tree.

Not wishing to place too much pressure on the young wolves, we very reluctantly returned to the office. We told staff members that we had only been there a few minutes and out they came. The people in the office told us that we had been very lucky to see the pups in such a short time and I guess we had been, but Jan's face told a different story. The look in her eyes as she gazed across at me, said that as far as she was concerned not all that had just happened was down to luck.

The pups were now spending a good deal of their time above ground. Warm summer days now encouraged them to rest in the shade of the great trees, rather than the cool earth of one of the many rendezvous sites (R.V.'s) situated around the wolves' territory.

The adults brought the young wolves items of interest to play with, trying to encourage them to work out the rank structure between themselves that will be so important to them as adults.

Before the young wolves were weaned the adults used mostly fur and feather to teach them. Already their games had taken on the familiar ranking system used by the adults. As the pups had not yet been named, we decided to give them our own names so we could identify them.

The battle for dominance usually took place between the girl pup we named Maggy and Jasper, the boldest boy pup, with the smaller of the two boys happy to watch just away from the other two. We named him Little Mo.

Maggy was always the biggest and boldest of the pups. Short for Magua her name means 'Bear', because of her remarkable likeness to a bear cub when she was younger.

She would growl and snap at Jasper as he tried to take her feather that had been presented by the adults. Rather than push his luck he would go over to Little Mo and the two of them would play happily while Maggy chewed her feather.

Slowly over the next couple of weeks, the feather and fur made way for food, firstly in the form of regurgitated meat and then chunks brought back to them in the mouths of the adults. Standing quite still to begin with, the adults encouraged the pups to take the food from them by leaving a small piece trailing from the mouth.

As you would expect, Maggy was the first to show for the food. Her boldness even surprised the adults who found they had to move their heads from side to side away from the young wolf, applying slightly more pressure than they did with the other two pups.

Each adult gave the young wolves their own individual lessons. Jasper, not quite so bold as his sister, took his food very gently from Daisy's mouth, with Little Mo happier to pick up his brother's leftovers rather than take his own food from the mouth of Lakota, his uncle.

Little Mo displayed all the behaviour of a low ranking wolf. We wondered if, as an adult, he would be destined to be the future Omega of the pack.

These early lessons are of great importance to the young wolves, teaching them how to defend their own individual piece of food.

I was once asked about my views on teaching the domestic dog using the wolf's behaviour. Using the wolf's language to break down communication barriers between our dogs and ourselves can be very useful. The more of their language we understand the less chance there is of confusion, both for ourselves and most importantly our pets.

However some of the wolves teachings would not be acceptable in our modern society. Food defence is one of them. As they grow, the adults increase the level of teaching among the pups, firstly by moving the young wolves' food around before they are allowed to take it, introducing them to hunting behaviour. After this the adults can be seen snatching the young wolves food back from them. Having chased it and then killed it, the pups must learn to defend their share of it.

The adults will successfully take food from the young maybe only once or twice before the pups switch on to the fact that they must defend what's theirs. Growling low, their tongues protruding through their bared teeth, the young wolves display all the defensive qualities of their adults.

Watching this type of behaviour, we are encouraged to take food and bones from our own dogs, thinking this will ensure that both ourselves and more importantly, our children, can approach the animal in safety when it is feeding. In fact we could not be more wrong. As we can now see, by removing the dog's food all that will be gained is that he or she will now be prepared to defend it.

Fortunately, in most cases there is an alternative. Only by modifying the wolf's own language are we able to use this communication. In the case of food, even an alpha will respect a lower rank when it is eating. Having taught the animal to defend, disciplining it for doing what it has been told would lead to confusion, weakening the all-important bonds between them.

Often I have approached a lower ranking wolf as it fed, testing its ability to defend. The animal will display all the defensive qualities it has been taught, but as a high ranking wolf it is my reaction to this display that matters; standing tall, stiff legged, muzzle high and eyes soft or blinking. With this display, I have just told this animal that I fully respect his or her defence but, I am higher ranking than he or she and I am staying right here until I decide it is time to leave.

Throughout this exchange I would constantly quote my alpha's rules, doing nothing he himself would not have done if he was there. Should I require his assistance in this situation I would simply call my leader and he would reinforce the same rules.

Again in most of our modern society this type of behaviour is not acceptable, but remember in the wolf's world a growl does not always symbolise that you will be bitten. Their world is made up of avoidance. The growl is the animal's way of avoiding conflict - it is a warning. It is your reaction to this warning that counts, backed up by the rank your dog thinks you hold, not the rank you think you hold with your dog.

In our world the better and safer option is to try to avoid these situations. In this case, a confrontation can easily be avoided by giving the animal something when you approach his bowl or bone, not taking it away. Take a handful of food from the young animal's bowl prior to placing it down and then offer it to the pup as it eats. By offering it food rather than taking it away you should cut down on the animal's defensive instincts.

Never forget the amount of teaching that is done around food as the tiny animal grows; when it feeds, where on the carcass it feeds and most importantly, which order it feeds in.

Another factor that could affect your domestic pet's stability is its acceptance into adulthood. From the time we bring our young pup home, the way we talk to it and the way we act around it all prepares it for adulthood, I believe that at least 30 to 40 percent of a domestic pups learning is through association. If the pup is left to play with children then its rate of maturity could slow to that of the child's or in some cases, the animal quickly discovers that it has matured faster and attempts to dominate the child.

As we have seen with the wolf pups, the squabbles among them help them to establish the social order that they take with them into adulthood. Once dominated, the dog will expect the child to fall in line with pack rules. You can now begin to see the importance of making the dog's rules and our own family rules the same.

As the puppy reaches the four-month stage many people look towards taking their young charge to puppy classes. This involves taking the young animal to an organised class where, more often than not, it meets with a group of other pups. This will teach the young dog how to behave around other pups and establish a rank structure based on the animals he encounters but, it will not always help the young animal mature.

In the wolf pack the juveniles often do this job, last year's pups that have now reached adulthood and already taken their place among the wolf's strict social structure. Using games and play the juveniles teach the young pups to accept their future within the pack, carefully watched by the adults who make sure pack rules are firmly but fairly taught.

If any of this seems strangely familiar then look no further than humans. The only difference is, as leaders we take on too much responsibility, involving ourselves in jobs that are not ours. As beta I was a mirrored version of my leader. His rules were my rules. He left me to enforce them whilst he led and guarded the pack. If he did not trust me to carry out his rules, then he would have to enforce them himself, leaving his position open. The wolf pack works on co-operation and trust, our own family packs (including our dogs) will also work on the same principle if we firstly teach and then trust in our animals to carry out our actions.

A woman once asked me why one of her dogs disciplined other people's animals when they jumped up at her? She herself had very well behaved dogs that had been taught her own pack rules, one of which was not to jump up. Living alone with her three family members, they had all formed a pack with her beta simply reinforcing her own rules whilst she led the pack. One of these rules was 'no jumping up'.

The wolves maturity is installed in them through association and patient teaching, in some cases, such as wolf packs that have to follow migratory herds, this can happen as early as six to nine months. With adulthood comes stability and a balance that, through modern society, our domestic dogs have sometimes come to lack in their education, making them difficult to train in certain aspects that only become apparent through the animals full development into adulthood.

The dawn chorus tells me once more that the sun is about to rise, bringing with it another warm summer's day. The wolves are already awake and on the move; they know today is feed day.

As the young wolves play in the tall grass, the early morning dew soaks their fur while the black shapes of the ravens who had provided my early wake up call, can be seen circling high above the trees.

According to Indian legend it was the raven who saved the world from darkness. A woman had stolen the sun and kept it rolled up in a bundle in her lodge. When the raven became old enough to play, he rolled the sun out of the door of the lodge and followed it. The raven then flew the sun up into the sky to light up the world. The sun was very heavy and the raven had to beat his wings very loudly to get into the air. His wings can still be heard to this day; every morning as the sun rises ravens' wings can be heard carrying it into the sky.

Ravens have also been known to call large predators such as bears, cougar and wolves to dead animals, knowing these animals will open up the carcass so that the ravens can feed from the scraps that are left. The connection between wolves and ravens again conjure up images of evil but, once more, we are guilty of simply misinterpreting the co-operation between two species willing to help each other's survival.

The pack begins to circle the trees. Smelling the fresh meat heightens their prey drive; even the pups know this unforgettable scent that now fills their territory. In the distance, the sound of the keepers' vehicles as they deliver the wolf's quarry can be heard. Entering their territory, the prey is moved around on the back of one of the vehicles.

Raising the wolves' prey drive even further is achieved by moving their food away from them or parallel to them. If more pressure is needed then we can zigzag the carcass but great care needs to be taken. By zigzagging their potential meal, the wolves are made to work a good deal harder for their food. Not only do they have to adjust their body position but they also have to adjust their bite. With the increase in movement the difficulty also lies in being able to locate and eventually grab one of the animal's flanks to bring it down. This diversionary tactic on the side of the quarry is often all that is needed to terminate the wolf's attack. Wolves, like most Canids, prefer to move in straight lines when hunting. The zigzag motion brings out the wolves' natural instinct to abandon the hunt in search of an easier meal.

Some friends of ours who use their dogs for agility brought this point home to us. They talked to us of problems they had with the weave pole, a discipline that involves the dog moving in and out of a straight line of poles placed 18 inches - 2 feet apart. The animals in question had exercised their natural instinct to terminate the chase when made to zigzag but, one more thing that seemed to arise time and again was, that the dogs that terminated more than any of the others were the animals that showed a lack of maturity. Their lack of teaching to adulthood was now beginning to affect the most important part of their wild relatives' survival. Their ability to hunt.

At the height of the wolves' prey drive their food is released and they move in, attacking flanks and the nose of their quarry. The wolves' hunting formation mimics that of their wild brothers. Even though the animal has long since been dead, the wolves' movement prior to the release of their meal encourages them to 'kill' their quarry before they eat.

Once the quarry is successfully killed, the wolves begin to once more reinforce the all-important rank structure that makes their feeding a strict social event. Using the same daily teachings, each wolf is reminded of their position within the pack.

Several metres away from the kill, the beta ranks weave their leaders' authority among the lower ranking wolves.

By the time they reach the kill, where their alphas will already be feeding, they will know when they can begin to eat and where on the kill they can position to feed. Leaving the alphas to take care of any testing that might come their way under the distraction of the food.

The alpha pairing normally position themselves either side of the rib cage, here they can gain access to the internal organs that contain most of the nutrients needed to maintain their leadership.

The betas will normally be positioned on the opposite side to the alphas, feeding on the rump and shoulder areas.

The remaining pack members will either be made to wait until the hierarchy has left the kill or they will be allowed to feast on the back and head area between the two betas.

Any pups are able to feed between their parents, where they too can take a small share of the valuable nutrients needed to build strong and healthy bones that will ensure the future of the pack.

The omega rank is often the only wolf who is made to wait until the end. This job requires him/her to be available should tensions get high around the kill. Omegas can often be seen approaching the kill and will appear to be chased off before they are able to feed, giving the impression to the outside world of bullying tactics by higher ranking wolves. This is often not the case, the omega rank moves to the feeding pack most of the time only to calm a situation that could possibly affect the wolves' harmony. Having placed itself between the offending animals, the omega then takes the discipline itself, cleverly using submissive and play behaviour that is unique to this rank. Uninjured and fully accepted by the remaining pack, the omega then returns to a position from which he/she can monitor the pack's activities.

Many of these food disputes come from young wolves who have not yet reached full adulthood, underlining once again the importance of maturity among the pack members. When every wolf has eaten and family bonds have been re-established, the pack seeks shade so they can rest after their feast.

Each adult wolf in our captive pack is fed a minimum of between four to six pounds of fresh meat per day on a feast and famine diet of between one and three days. That is an awfully large amount of food and it must have time to digest.

The wolves' rest enables other creatures that share their territory to roam among the forest relatively free from harm. Ravens come to feast on the remains of the wolves' meal. For animals such as squirrels and rabbits, it is a chance to forage among the grass for tender summer shoots and berries. Pheasants, too take advantage of the wolves' absence, carefully pecking in the tall grass. Only their heads can be seen occasionally appearing over the foliage, checking on the wolves' whereabouts.

At the age of six months, the three young wolves displayed all of their hunting ability. Led by the ever-watchful Maggy, the pups failed to show for a feed that had been brought to the pack. It was not only ourselves that showed concern, the adults too were equally uncertain about the young wolves' absence.

Leaving the kill, it was Two Crops, their older brother, who went looking for the pups. After only a few short moments, Two Crops returned with the three pups led of course by Maggy, frantically nibbling at the object he carried in his mouth. Two Crops paused by one of the large oak trees and placed the furry grey object on the ground between his outstretched paws.

Having now been firmly chastised by her elder brother for her persistence, Maggy was now on her side in front of Two Crops, showing him all the respect you would come to expect from a near adult animal.

Both Jasper and Mo had reached the remaining pack members, who were now making their way towards the spot where the two wolves were guarding their prize. The object that was creating all the excitement turned out to be a grey squirrel that had been caught by Maggy herself; this explained why she was so determined to get it back from Two Crops.

The two wolves were now on their feet as the remaining pack crowded around the very defensive Two Crops and his submissive younger sister. It was Zeva who eventually taught her daughter exactly how to get something that you have caught back from a much larger male. By creating an exchange of growls between two of the males in the pack, she distracted Two Crops just long enough for Zeva to move in and snatch the squirrel. Closely followed by Maggy, the two wolves ran into the trees where the young wolf's prize was returned to her.

Almost as if Zeva was giving her daughter a refresher in food defence, she remained by the young wolf's side as the pack once more crowded around them. Teeth bared, tongues protruding, the two wolves began to defend their kill. Backed up by her mother's support, Maggy now began to show the true potential of a wolf we all believe to be a future high-ranking female. Slowly Zeva moved back away from Maggy, leaving her to defend her own food. She had taught the young wolf a valuable lesson, probably one she would never forget.

Maggy with her prize.

CHAPTER 11

The arrival of Zarnesti and Dakota

August 5th 2001, Jan's birthday. The sun rising in the sky in front of us as we began our long journey would start a new day that was to change the rest of our lives. We were going to pick up two wolves that were going to be entrusted into our care. Zarnesti a European wolf that, having suffered a fractured jaw as a pup, had been cared for and raised by keepers who almost certainly saved his tiny life.

Zarnesti

Now, at the age of three months he and Dakota, a female timber wolf that he had formed such a close bond with, would together provide a pack security that would never challenge his disability.

Having met again with very close friends of ours that had cared for the two wolves' welfare, we began the long journey home. Gazing in through one of the many air-holes that ran around the wolves cargo crate, we were totally unaware of what great ambassadors the two animals who now lay peacefully resting in the dark comfort of the back of our vehicle would become.

In the next few months, both wolves joined us at the front of their enclosure every time we gave one of the many talks to students, the wolves' interactions with the team helping to dispel the many myths that surround wolves.

As a very high percentage of all wolf persecution is fear based, the need for wolves such as Zarnesti and Dakota has proved to be invaluable with the education of members of the general public, as well as enthusiasts of the species and related animals.

Dakota and Shaun

On several occasions the wolves have surprised even us. Sometimes we will give talks to the general public that visit the park. One such talk was for a large family of adults and teenage children.

Obviously interested in wolves, they asked us about the two animals that had now joined us as we spoke to them.

Between interacting with the two wolves, we managed to explain the importance of us trying to meet the wolves' requirements rather than them having to meet ours. We have always believed that the wolves, first and foremost, should be allowed to be wolves interacting with fellow pack members. If we wish to join this family than we must learn their ways, not subject them to ours.

At that moment Dakota left my side where she was busily transferring her scent to my clothing, despite the fact that I was already covered in her smell. She made her way over to where a very quiet man stood. He was part of the family we were talking to. For a few seconds man and wolf just stood there looking at one another. I had never seen this reaction in Dakota before, her actions puzzled me so much that I left Jan talking to the remainder of the family whilst I watched this exchange taking place. Slowly the gentleman moved slightly to his left. Dakota, not wishing the man to leave moved to her right, offering him the chance to play with her by bowing in front of him. A large smile immediately came to the man's face, I can remember thinking that the lips drawn back in a smile rather than raised, also tells the wolves that it is time to play. Unaware that his happiness was all that was needed for Dakota to

continue, the pair of them spent many minutes exchanging play gestures before the gentleman grew tired. She returned to my side and after asking my permission to greet me, her leader, she licked at my face before moving away.

Our wolves are always free to interact with team members or not as they choose, no restrictions are ever placed on their natural communication with their fellow pack mates or us. By this time Dakota's playmate had rejoined his family saying nothing, he simply watched the two wolves as they disappeared off into the trees. I apologised to the entire family for having to leave them but, I had a small group of school children who had come to hear us talk about the wolves. Explaining that I was happy to leave them in Jan's capable hands if they had any more questions that they needed answering, I bid them good-bye.

After some time Jan came over to where I had just finished talking to the children. She had spent nearly an hour chatting to the family of people, where she had discovered that the gentleman that had found a new playmate in Dakota had in fact found a great deal more from her friendship. Several months ago this gentleman had suffered a severe stroke, leaving him near disabled, having always lived an active lifestyle through his work and the sports he loved so much. His family feared that he had lost his will to come through something that most of us could not even imagine. Having always enjoyed visiting with the animals, this was one of the only things left for them to try. After moving this giant of a man to tears, Dakota had touched him so deeply that he had found in her his will to carry on. This same man and his family now travel many miles just to visit with her and every time she still gives him the same playful greeting.

A similar story happened to Zarnesti when he was just a pup. The wolves and ourselves had visitors in the form of a family who had brought their disabled son to visit the animals. Instantly Zarnesti and the young lad connected, exchanging facial greetings with one another, they communicated for what must have been twenty or thirty minutes. The look of sheer happiness on this young boy's face as he talked to Zarnesti moved us all. As I sat there looking around at the rest of the team watching them desperately trying to fight back the tears of happiness that now filled their eyes. I could not help thinking to myself that if nothing else came of the time we spend with our two wolves, these two remarkable stories will stay with us all forever, making our work all the more worthwhile.

Over the next few months the bond between Zarnesti, Dakota and ourselves grew stronger and stronger. Constantly teaching me their ways I have come to realise all that these magnificent creatures stand for. Trust, loyalty, pack survival and most importantly family. Every day that I spend with them holds a deeper respect for this animal that I am proud to call family.

Dakota and Zarnesti

12

Daisy's story - part 2

Summer is now in full swing; birds fly back and forth to their young taking care of their never-ending duties to feed them. Once again Old Hollow has provided warm dry shelter for the two tawny owls and the latest batch of offspring that now frantically call to their parents for food. Fortunately the constant early rain has not effected the rodent population and the two owls fly back and forth over my head with a constant stream of food for their young.

The mice and voles not only provide the owls with food; in the distance a dog fox pounces on the tall thickets of grass, his keen hearing can pick out the tiny rustling sounds made by the rodents as they travel along their maze of underground tunnels.

As dawn breaks overhead a kestrel hovers, its keen eyesight able to pick up the slightest movements that could mean a meal for its waiting young.

Surrounded by all of nature's creatures undertaking their daily duties, it is easy for me to loose touch with both the work that I am undertaking and the reality of the outside world. I rely on messages sent from home to keep in touch with world events and the rapid growth of our children who now insist on telling their friends that their daddy lives with wolves.

To my front, the now eight month old pups play among the adults in the clearing of the trees where I have watched them so many times before. Maggy still continues to dominate her two brothers, but they now stand tall above their sister.

Even little Mo, so tiny as a pup, now looks every inch an adult, his nature still remains the only give-away that he was once so young and defenceless in the presence of the adults and his litter mates.

Jasper has turned into a fine young adult, as I watch he pins his brother and stands over him, rolling him on to his back. The ease with which Mo displays his vulnerable underside is not all contributed to Jasper's strength, the submissive nature of his brother accounting largely for his dominant stance.

Zeva (their mother) has raised her pups through their first few vulnerable months of life. She was assisted, from when they were three months old, by Two Crops their older brother but, the credit for their educated rise into adulthood must lay with the tender patient teachings of their nanny, Daisy.

From her fight for life eighteen months ago Daisy has raised yet another generation of wolves into the world. It is more than likely her experience, that was largely responsible for saving the young wolves lives during the tremendous storm that flooded their den, when they were just tiny pups. Under Daisy's' guidance they have learnt how to protect themselves, both from rival wolves and the attentions of higher ranking pack members.

They can now hunt to feed themselves and their family and most importantly, they are now able to defend their own food under the most extreme conditions. They have learnt the language, behaviour and true ways of the wolf, from one of the finest teachers we have had the pleasure of knowing during our time with these animals.

When they reached nearly nine months of age, Daisy's work with her charges was finished, she had taught them all she could. Now Maggy, Jasper and Mo must make their own ways through life, taking their rightful places within the pack's social structure.

As if she were following some primitive instinct, that now told her that it was time to rest. Daisy said her final good-bye to the family that she had cared for and protected her entire life. At the age of sixteen she had made sure the pups in her care had safely reached adulthood before she sadly died. Found laying under the very same Oak tree from where she had watched over the many generations of pups in her care, she had peacefully laid down to finally rest her tired body.

I took great comfort in the fact that Daisy had not suffered. Nature has a way of doing this among the wolves. Seeming to understand the high level of pride that comes with wild animals, the wolves end comes with total preservation of their dignity, never having to undergo prolonged suffering.

Having made the phone call back to the team, telling them that Daisy had gone, I made arrangements to help the pack restructure once more. As I waited for nightfall I began to reflect on Daisy's life.

I regret that I had not known her as a pup, only the adult that she had come to be. Loyalty, teacher and total devotion to her family were among some of the many qualities that had made her such an obvious choice for the job she loved so much, the pup's nanny.

For the team and maybe the wolves themselves, life within the pack would not be the same now that Daisy was gone. As the first calls from the pack rang out across the valley, I finally realised that her distinctive howl would never again be heard echoing through the trees that she had so protectively called home.

Tonight, even the wolves as they called, seemed different. Sitting there in the darkness that I had come to know so well from living with the wolves, I remembered how intense Daisy's teaching of the young pup we called Maggy had been, along with Two Crops, who had helped her with the pups upbringing from three months of age.

Was her increase in teaching simply to educate the two inexperienced young animals or was she training her own replacement?

Getting warily to my feet I had decided that my last tribute to Daisy would be to provide the voice of the lone wolf that would now help her pack restructure. As I began to call back into the night I remembered the words of an Indian tribal elder, told to one of my teachers. He said that something has only died when it has been forgotten, as long as someone remembers them, then the spirit will always remain with you.

If the words of these people that I hold in great respect are so, then there is not a day that goes by where we do not think of the wolf that we had come to call 'Nanny'.

Daisy

13

A wolf man is born

Largely due to the extensive media coverage we received from our unusual work with the wolves, we have found out that there is a great amount of interest in these animals. Having already recorded a small amount of our work on a television programme that featured life around the animals at the park, we were invited to attend a morning radio show to help launch its first showing.

The interview began and ended with me in full cry, offering my host a rallying howl. It was then that I began to realise, by the startled look on his face and the fact that he had now moved his chair back at least three feet, that not all of our new found popularity was down to the wolves.

I had left Jan outside sitting among other guests who had been invited down to talk on a variety of different subjects. Unaware that these people could hear every word from the show, including my wolf calls, I returned to where Jan and two other guests were seated. The look on her face was one that I recognised from past experiences! As we left the room she explained that my calling had left the two elderly women somewhat shaken. Believing that I had a wolf in the studio, they were quite concerned for their own safety. They wanted to know which way I was going to bring this animal out. Jan reassured the two ladies in her company that, even if there was an actual wolf in the studio, they would have little to fear as the animal would be far more apprehensive of them then they would of it. She went on to explain that it was in fact me that was making these calls rather than a real wolf.

On our way back to the vehicle we were stopped by a very breathless lady from the offices, who had ran to catch us before we left. She stated that one of her colleagues had heard the interview on his way into the studio and wondered if we would mind waiting to talk to him regarding our work with the wolves.

These first two interviews were to be the start of many that we did over a two-week period. Our time was spent racing from one part of the country to the other, whilst maintaining the wolf pack management programmes, giving interviews by phone as we travelled.

As I drove, Jan would arrange a schedule that would cover our talk time whilst at the same time not interfering with our time with the wolves. Covering everything from how we started the breeding programmes to our time actually living with the wolves, Jan even covered one interview over the phone as to our own personal 'breeding programme'. As you can imagine this interview involved a lot of 'no comments' and a questioning look when she finally managed to get off the phone!

'The wolf man is on his way to you now,' the keepers would announce to one another, as I travelled through the park on the way to the wolves. This was a name that was picked up on by the media and used on a regular basis. The story of the wolf man told to me by my teachers is a good deal more saddening.

Once (long ago) a man had two very bad wives. Thinking that their lack of shame was a result of the people around them, he decided to move them to a place where they had no one to talk to and no one to see. Near to where they now camped was a small hill where the man would sit daily, in quiet contemplation, on an old buffalo skull.

Every evening at sundown, the man would walk to the top of the hill, where he would watch for the buffalo feeding and spot any of his enemies that may be close by. In their husband's absence, the two women talked of their now lonely life with no one to talk to and no one to visit.

They decided to kill their husband, so they could return to their relatives and once more have a good time. As their husband set off to hunt, the two women went to the top of the hill to the skull of the buffalo where their husband would sit. There, they dug a deep pit, which they covered with sticks and leaves. They then placed the skull carefully on top of their trap.

Late that afternoon, they saw their husband returning; laden down with fresh meat and they hastened to cook for him. After eating, he walked up to the top of the hill as usual and sat down on the skull. The thin sticks instantly gave way and the man fell into the pit. Having seen their husband disappear, the two women quickly dismantled their lodge, packed their belongings and moved back to the main camp.

When they got close enough to the camp for the people to hear them, they began to cry and mourn.

'Why do you cry and mourn?' asked the villagers. 'And where is your husband?' The two women wept again and said that he had been out hunting but had not returned. They feared he was dead.

The man had been badly hurt when he had fallen into the pit. He was too bruised to move, let alone climb out. A travelling wolf heard the man and pitied him. With a very loud howl, the wolf called to his friends. When the other wolves heard the pack member, they ran quickly to join him, they also brought with them a badger, a coyote and a fox.

'In this hole lies a fallen man,' said wolf. 'He is my find, so myself and the oldest wolves will have him as our brother.' The rest of the animals agreed with the wolf and began to dig a hole beside the man.

The wolf spoke again and this time said 'This man will be brother to us all but, he is my find and will therefore live with me.' The wolf then jumped into the hole and dragged the man out.

He was taken to the elder of the wolf people where he was given powerful medicine and fed with nourishing kidney. His hands and head were made to look like those of the wolves.

The people of this time used to make holes in the cave walls and set snares for the wolves and other creatures when they came to eat the meat. One night the wolves went to eat the meat from the snares.

'Wait here,' said the wolf man, 'I will fix the snares so you will not be caught.' He went on and fixed all of the traps before calling the wolves and other animals down to feed. In the morning the villagers were surprised that all their snares had been sprung and yet not a single animal had been caught.

For many nights, the villagers wires were drawn out and their meat gone, until one night the wolves went down to feed, only to find that the only meat that had been left was a rotten bull. Angry, the wolf man cried out into the night.

The people heard him and said 'It is a man wolf who has done this. We will catch him.' They went down and replaced the rotten bull with good quality food and waited for the wolves to come.

That night the wolves returned and with them came the man wolf. Seeing the fresh meat, he ran forwards to eat. The villagers rushed forward and caught him in their ropes. They then took him to their lodge. When they could see clearly in the firelight, they instantly recognised the man as the one who had been lost.

'No' said the man, 'I was not lost; my wives tried to kill me. They dug a pit for me to fall into. I was badly hurt and could not get out. The wolves took pity on me and rescued me. Without their help, I would have certainly died.'

When the villagers heard this they were very angry. The two women were handed over to the 'Warriors' Society' that dealt out punishment for crimes against tribal members. After that night the two women were never seen again.

As I travel through the park to the wolves, I still hear mention of the name wolf man to announce my arrival. The picture that is often conjured up by this name will hopefully soon be consigned to the past.

In the future, one of our aims is to dispel the image of half man half animal capable of killing anything it comes into contact with. This is not the wolf. Instead from now on it is more helpful to think of the name 'wolf man' as merely a way of describing one man's fight to help save the animals he has come to call family.

Fortunately, over the years I have had the chance to dispel many of the tags I received in the early days, regarding my sanity. People are now starting to see the advantages of learning from the wolves themselves.

However, learning can often mean great sacrifice on the part of the person who is being taught. My only advice to anyone wishing to begin or continue working with wolves is to never give up. You can rest assured that the animals that you work with have never given up in their lives. Watch them and learn from them and they will always provide you with enough strength to face whatever life may throw at you.

One story that always springs to mind, as I remember about the times when I would rather have been somewhere else, starts when I was out with the wolves updating my recordings of their howls to use with other packs…

All of my equipment was meant to be portable and easy to carry. However in order for me to receive the wolves' howls at great distances, I had made a receiver dish out of an old discarded satellite dish. I had begged the dish from an electrical shop, following the replacement of the old dishes with an updated version. The dish and its stand (created from an old microphone stand) was by no means easily portable, it was more accurate to say that it could be just about carried by one person - with difficulty!

Having staggered down to the position from which I would make my recordings, I set up the dish and waited for the first calls from the wolves. I sat beneath what little shelter the trees afforded me, having lost all of their leaves to the bitter autumn winds. The rain had soaked me through to the skin in just the few minutes that it had taken me to walk down to the small copse. The wind was blowing directly into my face, making my cheeks burn with the mixture of wind and rain.

Then, a very familiar and welcome scent entered my nostrils. If I was not mistaken, it was the unforgettable smell of beer! I quickly dismissed this as wishful thinking, deciding that my nose was playing tricks on me. After all, it was Saturday night and many normal people would in fact be out enjoying the odd pint.

Suddenly, my train of thought was broken by the sound of the wolves who now began to howl. With my hands shaking from the bitter cold, I just about managed to press the record button on my tape machine.

Keeping perfectly still, I had to be careful not to make any sound that would not be forgiven by the sensitive microphone pointing at the large dish. I required it to pick up sounds that only the dish and the surrounding animals and birds could hear. I was ever optimistic as to what I would actually record: planes, helicopters and all kinds of neighbouring wildlife, to name just a few possibilities.

As the wolves' howl faded, I played back my recordings to see what I had and if I needed to make any adjustments to the dish. It was at this point that I made an amazing discovery. It seemed as if the wolves' howling was being accompanied by music. The music, I later discovered from the children, was a track by Sonique. Due to the wind direction my recording equipment had picked up music from a neighbouring nightclub! I had learnt two things that night. One was that the wolves must be aware of a great deal of activity through the sounds from the surrounding civilisation, often from several miles away. The other was that my time with the wolves had taught me that I now possessed the ability to smell beer from several hundred metres away, when the wind is right!

CHAPTER 14

Howl-ins

Peoples' misconceptions and fears of wolves are of concern to everyone who has ever worked with or been involved in the welfare of these animals. This is one of the reasons why we introduced the 'Howl-ins.'

The usual reaction from people if they are scared of something is to try to destroy it. Held at Longleat Safari Park in Wiltshire, these howl-ins provide adults and children of all ages with a chance to spend time in the company of wolves.

Dakota howling

Nightfall with the wolves is a truly magical time and hearing the wolves howl for the first time is like experiencing the opera for the first time. You never really know what a person's reaction is going to be until they have heard it.

On the many nights we spent with the wolves calling back and forth to one another, people passing would ask us if they could stay a while and listen. The popularity of what we were doing finally persuaded us to share our experiences with others.

From the research that we had done with them so far, we knew that communicating with the wolves would be good for their natural behaviour. Hopefully we could now use these calls to educate people and help them understand one of the things that they fear about the wolves most, their spine chilling howl. Heard within nearly every horror movie that has ever been made, the calling of wolves has not helped in the quest to improve their popularity. However now, through these howl-ins we can help to teach the general public the true meanings of this unforgettable language.

Seven o'clock in the evening; the cool night air has met with the warmth of the day causing the Leat to release a thin layer of mist over its waters, as dusk now leads us gently from day into night.

Jan and I stand in the car park awaiting the arrival of a small group of people. They have come to hear one of nature's most powerful voices – that of the wolf.

Filled with both apprehension and excitement we begin to lead the four adults and two children along the path to the edge of the vast Longleat forest. Here just inside the tree line, under the comfort of one of the many giant trees, I begin to talk of the animals that we have become so close to.

With the exchange of information and questions from their inquiring minds, the previously wary audience already began to understand a little more than they had a few minutes ago. I explained what they were about to hear and how each rank differs slightly from the next. (The individual wolves' voices match the rank they currently occupy). Everybody now anticipates with excitement the sound that is to shortly fill their sense of hearing. As usual with talks like these, we ask the people, for the next few minutes, to forget all sense but one - that of sound.

The darkness has now replaced the twilight. Everything has been explained, all that is now left for these people is to listen to and enjoy the wolves' calls.

Leaving the group briefly, both Jan and myself move slightly up the track. After two deep breaths, I call out to the wolves, telling them that I am rallying my pack to within an uncomfortable distance to their territory. My howl begins slowly and is purposely lacking slightly in confidence. I howl three times before being joined by Jan. Growing now in confidence we both increase the intensity of our howls.

From within their territory the wolves would now see this as a serious challenge. Their reply should soon fill the crystal clear night air. Suddenly the darkness becomes alive with the impressive sound of a complete pack of wolves, every rank announcing its presence and a willingness to defend what it has.

Jan and I return to the group who by now are totally engrossed in the sound of the wolves. I watch the children's' faces as they listen. They are our future and will grow up with a totally impartial view of the creatures that share our world. Giving them the true story of the wolf will help them and us to secure a future for our fellow animals. Who knows? Their children and children's children may one day, once more, grow up with wild wolves roaming certain areas of our countryside.

The cries that have provided the children and adults with the smiles that now light up their faces have ceased. Their reaction needs no words, it is clear from everybody's expressions, the joy they have taken from their experience.

As the mid-ranking wolves' howl is to try to create the illusion of numbers among the pack, we ask the group to guess how many wolves they believe to have been calling to them. The lowest number we are given is ten. There were in fact only five wolves making their defence. This shows how effective, even to our ears, this middle rank can be.

From the unknown to total regard for the wolf in just over an hour, these six people have spent part of their evening in the company of the wolves. They leave with a different and deeper understanding and with a lot less fear of the wolf.

CHAPTER 15

Reuben's story

Meeting Reuben for the first time was a completely different adventure for me. Being possibly the oldest wolf that I have worked with for a long time, he was truly remarkable. Despite being partially sighted, he travelled around very well, pacing himself to meet the requirements of the day. The remarkable side of Reuben's nature is revealed in the fact that despite his physical disadvantages, he still managed to hold the rank of beta within the pack. Reuben's health and quality of life are a credit to the keepers who cared for his welfare; everything else is down to the wolf himself.

At nearly 17 years of age, Reuben became my teacher when I became part of his wolf pack. Over the first few months, this animal of great experience would guide me through the many duties that he had to perform as beta male.

Many people believe that the alpha pairing are the two wolves that lead the pack, this is true to a certain extent but, as you will now see, the alphas' leadership is only ever as good as their betas.

It is the job of the alphas to guide, protect and breed for the entire pack. Together they teach and reinforce pack rules on a daily basis. The duties of maintaining leadership through food management and a balanced domination of every wolf under their care, along with defending the pack and its territory, would require more hours in the day than the wolves actually have. This is where a good beta comes in. Carefully chosen in the beginning, this animal is then taught to be an extension of its leaders.

Reuben was an exceptional beta, a complete mirror image of his alphas. Their rules were his rules. Many times a day he would remind and guide me through exactly what was required from the lower ranking wolves. This included where and how they rested, places and occasions they could scent, also who needed to be asked before they could greet their leaders. Testing by lower ranking wolves was dealt with correctly and fairly, as was most importantly, enforcing and maintaining a strict social structure around the kill.

The wolves' ranking system is not unlike our own working environment. Each wolf is expected to teach and guide the next rank down, not only through the job that they currently hold but also in preparation for the rank they eventually hope to gain. The only significant difference is the final goal. Ours is to perform a service or to make a product to use in conjunction with our lifestyle; theirs is for pack security and future survival.

Within the wolf family we work hard on the small details, trying not to let them escalate into bigger, more complex problems that could all too easily weaken pack bonds and the all-important trust.

For the first few seconds after settling down to rest, each wolf has his or her own position. As a mid-high rank and next in line to Reuben, my initial resting position was to only show a small amount of underside, with my body slightly over to one side.

My alphas showed no underside at all, adopting a sphinx like posture, whereas the lower ranks were mostly governed not by position but by the distance they were from their leaders.

After these initial few seconds we would normally adopt one of three resting positions: the alert position (much the same as the sphinx posture that I described earlier), the circular position - with tail curled up across the nose to protect from the cold or, stretched out - allowing excess heat to filter from the body through the many sweat glands that the wolves have; all helping to place their scent around their territory.

Every time wolves run or play, their body temperature rises, releasing valuable scent into the air; this gives neighbouring packs valuable information on the mood and general morale of the pack.

When the kill was brought into the wolves I took my position as every other pack member. To an outsider we may have appeared to be running in no set pattern. In fact every move was very well rehearsed through constant hunt training. The idea being to cut off any escape that the animal may have, whilst resting each pack member to ensure that when the kill was made, a balance of strength from the males and speed from the females was always available.

At this point, in the wild, the wolves would have been prepared for a long siege between themselves and an animal that may outweigh them by a thousand pounds. The siege may sometimes last many days before the quarry would be weak enough to be brought to the ground and killed.

This type of kill can look very cruel to the outside world with the animal seeming to be eaten as it stands. In fact the wolves kill their prey very quickly. The only difference is that predators such as big cats often use suffocation or strangulation, making their kill appear more humane than that of the Canids.

To return to my own pack, once the kill was down and the keepers had left, a combination of strength and speed from the pack members would ensure that the kill was motionless. Reuben and the two alphas would come together for the all-important bonding prior to feeding. Their excitement at the prospect of food could sometimes stretch family ties to the limits. Meanwhile, the low ranking animals would form small groups based on their rank. Minor squabbles occurred as testing began, with lower ranking individuals looking for the possibility of weakness in higher ranking wolves, detection of these weaknesses could give them access to a better quality of food.

As part of their family and head of the middle ranks, I received a good deal of attention at this time. With a combination of young wolves just beginning to make their way through the rank system and old wolves who have been ousted from high positions, the entire mid ranks could be very unstable. The older wolves were more stable around the kill; having once held a position among the pack's hierarchy, they had a high degree of maturity making them quite balanced around food but, they would increase their testing during the breeding season.

My testing came from the younger wolves not yet sufficiently mature to deal with the distraction of food. Using a low growl I warned all those around me that I was prepared to defend my position. Any other testing would be dealt with by a facial display, raising the lips upwards to expose the teeth and most importantly, the large canines that can prove to be so intimidating to low ranking animals.

Normally this degree of discipline is all that is needed to deter would-be challengers but, if they are persistent, muzzling the offender will certainly dampen his enthusiasm. One of the highest forms of discipline among the wolves, muzzling is very effective. Short, sharp and straight to the point, this action involves covering the offending wolf's muzzle with yours and squeezing at varying pressures based on the severity of the offence.

In my position over this small group of relatively unbalanced animals, I had to use these disciplines often to maintain pack rules.

Reading this, you may have recognised this behaviour in your own dogs. This is why I believe that, because of the impression we give domestic dogs through the nature of our training, our own pack rules involve us leading a small group of mid ranking animals, (often because of their lack of maturity), with the human as either a mid-high rank or possibly (in some cases of experienced owners), their beta.

Knowing what it now involves, wouldn't you agree with me that, we are more likened to the mid-high rank and beta than we ever are an alpha?

Even in the uncertain middle ground of my pack's overall structure we still maintained the wolves' ways of teaching. Subdominant animals were expected to teach the ranks below and, by the time that my beta arrived, I had maintained the discipline that would now be required at the kill.

As we greeted, an exchange of testing took place. Everything turned to strength and the awesome power of these animals could now be felt as it took much of my own strength to push back against their heads and bodies.

If I was to maintain my position and safety amongst the wolves, I now had to compete with and better their testing of food dominance. Down on all fours in order to steady my position, I used my weight advantage among the wolves, pushing their heads away with mine and using my body to move them in the direction I now wanted them to go. The frantic licking of both Reuben's and my own muzzle now told us that it was time to move to the kill and join the alpha pairing to feed.

With our leaders in place and my beta feeding at the rump of our quarry, I moved to the shoulder from where I could hold my rank. I feel it is important at this stage to explain that I do not actually feast on the raw meat! To defend one's place seems to be enough. However I do remove the area of food that my rank entitles me to, ensuring that the pack's structure is not affected by my lack of appetite for their cuisine.

Once, when I first began interacting with the wolves, I found myself in what seemed to be a no win situation. Both Jan and myself were demonstrating the importance of food defence among the wolves to about twenty students. They were watching from outside the enclosure and I was inside, just back from where the wolves were eating. It was whilst explaining the significance of this type of feeding and the food they had to eat that the following strange encounter took place.

As I sat on a fallen log the alpha male, having finished eating came over to me carrying a front leg from the quarry in his mouth. Thinking he was going to cache the food for later consumption, I took little notice at first, but as he came and placed the food down between my feet it was clear that the leg was being offered to me. I am still not sure whether, at this stage, my lack of knowledge of their language had brought out his parental instinct to feed me as he would his own pups. All I knew was that, in front of me was this large impressive animal waiting expectantly for the instinct in me to kick in so that I would begin to feed. I realised I had two options. One, I could risk offending him and ignore the offering in front of me or two, I could feed on the leg and risk appearing on the front cover of most of the national newspapers.

I waited to see if he would after a while, just leave, thus resolving the problem, but this seemed to make the situation worse. The alpha decided that my hesitation showed that I needed more of an incentive and he proceeded to push the leg closer to me with his nose.

I eventually resolved the problem by picking up the food and holding it. Feeling satisfied that I would now feed the wolf left to rejoin the rest of the pack.

Being surrounded by hungry mouths on both sides underlines the importance of the earlier test of strength. If you get pushed from the position that you now protect, it will cut down on the amount of food that you will eat and so the decline in your health and fitness begins.

During the short time I had in Reuben's care he taught me a great deal about my future role as a beta rank. Sadly, his death was at the centre of a number of losses suffered at the park.

Having arrived as a litter and with a lack of pups in recent years, the wolf pack's age was now beginning to catch up with them. The pack was now down to three: Zac, Sheba and myself. Together we still defended and fed as a family but in light of the losses there was a definite need to produce a future generation.

We feared that the wolves' lack of breeding was down to Sheba and after testing her fertility, it was agreed that a new female should be introduced to the pack.

Introduction of wolves to an already established pack is not without its risks, as many people have discovered over the years. The ousting of the wolf by the pack, or them simply driving it away as it is introduced, has been known to cause serious injury to the animal, in some cases even death. We feel that this is largely due to the fact that a current pack member already takes the rank of the introduced animal. This causes the pack, under the direction of the challenged wolf, to drive the outsider away.

A lone wolf wishing to be allowed to join the security of a pack must wait to hear if there is a vacancy among the resident neighbouring wolves. Now, using the wolves' own techniques once more, we attempted to insert an outside wolf into the pack. Because the infiltration largely begins through sound, this was where we would start.

Soon after the resident pack had suffered their losses we began to use the howls of our rival wolves to apply slightly increased pressure to the pack. Now on the inside, I could see firsthand how this slow possible take-over of territory affects the wolves. We still defended, but my leaders would call both day and night, seeming to sense our vulnerability, as if waiting for the sound that would eventually come to help them.

Training the wolf who would give them this help had been going on now for one and a half months. We taught and encouraged the female to accept the high rank that would become vacant over the next few days. She had also been fed a very high quality of food and had begun to show all the trademarks of her new status. Her coat pattern had become bold to underline all the areas a wolf needs to communicate with other wolves. Her howl had become that of a high ranking animal and she displayed a dragging action whilst urinating. She was now ready to offer the resident pack their one chance to hold on to their territory.

The wolf's howl was recorded to give the illusion of distance, allowing us to work in metres whilst the sound we played to the pack would give the equivalent in miles. The wolves and I were just beginning to practice hunting techniques when the challenges began.

At first, rival packs called to one another, eventually directing their attention to us. As their howls faded we began to reply to the challenge. I crouched between Zac and Sheba, carefully blending my howl with theirs to slightly overlap. In the absence of a middle rank it proved to be a good deterrent, helping to slow the rival wolves' advances. Then, as we stopped, came the calls of our saviour, like the horn of the cavalry that had arrived just in time. Each one of us paused from the bonding that had taken place after our howl and listened. Lasting for a few seconds, her calls brought instant excitement to the pack. Using the high pitched whimper, Zac called us back together and using the same formation we began to call for her again. Our leaders' first few important howls tell us if we are to call or defend and this was most definitely a call.

The idea was to introduce both the lone wolf and our resident pack together by use of sound. With the Longleat pack we had applied pressure to the wolves by using the lone wolf. This was done without her actually occupying that pack, enabling a younger female to take the position. Now the use of this rogue animal would be to increase numbers, to actually become part of our wolf family. We would monitor the calls of both the lone wolf and the pack to establish the correct time of infiltration.

Over the next few nights the resident wolves, rival packs and this single wolf continued to communicate the ingredients of an eventual cocktail that would bring them together as one family. From within the resident pack, their callings had already begun to create a gap. Sheba, who had led the wolves as alpha female, slowly began to accept the role of beta. Changing her own sound and length of call, she stood close by me as she howled, leaving only Zac to pause between our cries to establish whether or not our defence was working.

From outside the pack's territory, the lone wolf observed by Jan and encouraged by the pack's calls, steadily moved closer. The ever-decreasing distance between them was also now beginning to change her own howl as she adopted the characteristic intermittent call of the alpha leadership.

The resident pack, this one single animal and myself had begun to form a family from several miles away. Using nothing but sound, we had introduced ourselves to each other and discovered a mutual security that she and the pack now so badly needed.

Both myself and the rest of the team could only watch in total amazement at seeing firsthand the way in which these incredible animals had now come together, using nothing but a trust in their own ancient language. Their future survival depended on them joining together as one pack.

Now they were showing signs of territorial defence, the time had come to see if their calls had worked. The rival wolves who had provided the need to increase numbers had all but finished their job and were now being moved steadily back, giving the newly formed pack the idea that together they were more than capable of defending their own piece of ground. It is this type of pressure that helps forge the lifelong bonds that hold the wolves together as a family.

In the past it would have taken several months to introduce another wolf into a captive pack, running the wolves side by side for long periods of time and still having to deal with heightened tension among the animals when they were finally introduced. Using their own communication techniques, it had taken a matter of days.

After the initial introductions through sound we then used scent, which had been collected from the new alpha female and sprayed just inside and outside their territory, carefully trying to symbolise the natural interaction between the two of them. Scenting and then returning to these sites helped the lone wolf to gather the final valuable information that would be left on and around her own odour by the resident pack. This would tell her whether it was safe for her to join them or not.

Last in the wolves' identification of status comes the use of sight. The bold markings that often denote a high rank are not always totally visible (particularly with the wolves' eyesight) when their first meeting takes place. The markings will fully form once the pack has settled down over the next few weeks. However, the combination of the other two factors and the decrease in the old female's markings seems to be sufficient for them to join without conflict, possibly because of the lack of importance the wolves' place on sight.

With a final exchange of communication between the two of them reinforcing their newfound bond (similar to that of a pack member returning) it was now time for them to come together. The excitement among the wolves and myself at this time was incredible, each of us reinforcing pack bonds, re-establishing rank status and laying scent around the boundary to our territory.

Once released, our new alpha made straight for Sheba, totally ignoring both Zac and myself. After a brief exchange of dominance, involving T'ing, (this entails of the blocking of your subdominant's path with your body), the new alpha female placed her head and front legs across the shoulders of her beta. Sheba lowered herself, accepting her new leader's status. In just a few seconds, the entire encounter had finished. All the long-range communication between them had cemented their bonds long before they had ever seen each other. Who says blind dates do not work?

Now, with her position clearly enforced, our new alpha moved to where Zac and I had been observing the encounter. She lowered herself slightly as she approached her leader, showing him the correct respect, but also very aware of Sheba's presence. Allowing him to sniff at her, she remained motionless aside from the odd quick twitch of her posture as he moved from one part of her body to another.

Having satisfied himself with her smell, Zac moved away. Our new family member then turned her attention towards me. Despite the fact that she had not seen me before, only my smell and sound had told her that this human was part of the pack, she showed no hesitation in her approach towards me. My beta rank enabled her to greet me and exchange scent, which was done by the rubbing of both body and head, transferring scent from one to the other, blending hers with mine. As alpha female she would need to be completely familiar with the smell of each and every pack member.

Having firmly established rank structure, our new leader now set off to establish her scent in and around her new territory. In light of the presence of outside packs, this merging of ground scent is very important. It informs rivals that this pack is once more able to defend the territory they have fought so hard to keep.

As for me, I had just had the privilege of being a part of one of the many marvels that make the natural world such a wonderful place to be, especially when your family happens to be that of one of her most legendary creatures, the wolf.

This wolf pack, as many others we have had the pleasure to live and work with, has like all their ancestors both wild and captive before them, come through tremendous losses, but through it all they have now emerged to find new hope. The introduction of this one animal should ensure their captive future, let's just hope that the knowledge we have gained from them will help to ensure the future of their wild brothers.

The Nez Percè

Throughout this book I have constantly made reference to the people who have inspired me to carry out my work with the wolves. Among some of the Native Americans with whom I have had the privilege to work, the small group of Nez Percè stays with me the most.

These proud people, who have become legendary for their close connection with the animals that share their lands, have helped people such as myself for centuries. Even though they have not actively been involved in our research, they have contributed greatly to the passion and understanding that I have towards the wolves and their future. I feel that to write this book without mentioning the history of the Nez Percè would be a great disappointment to its readers. Therefore, I would like to also take this opportunity to personally thank these people; in the very short time I have known them, their influence and wise words have come to guide me in my daily research and studies.

Living in the region of the Great Basin (Idaho, Oregon and Washington) and speaking Sahaptin (Penutian) the Nez Percè faced the harsh North American winters living in simple plains tipis. Their name of Nez Percè was given to them because when they were first encountered by the French, some members of the tribe were seen to be wearing pendants attached to their pierced noses.

Hunting wild game, in particular buffalo and salmon, these hardy people have always lived by nature's rules. The Nez Percè have generally had good relations with the white man, beginning with the French and then continuing with the Americans, such as Lewis and Clark, who in 1831 sent emissaries to St Louis requesting Christian missionaries.

During the region's Indian wars the Nez Percè remained neutral, this included the Rouge River Wars of the 1850's. When the great valleys and forest of the North West next saw war, the Nez Percè would write what was to be one of the greatest epics in the history of the entire Indian wars and would see the rise to national prominence of one of the greatest Indian leaders of all time.

The tribe was in fact two tribes, the Upper and Lower Nez Percè with each occupying its own lands but sharing common hunting grounds. This co-existence was lost however to the United States government in 1863 when a treaty between them and the Upper Nez Percè signed over both lands of the Nez Percè group and moved to another home, the Lapwai Reservation.

It had taken nearly ten years before the white mans' population growth in the Nez Percè territory reached a level where it would encroach on the Indians who were still refusing to abide by the treaty that had been signed on their behalf. Although the white sentiment did in fact support the creation of a lower Nez Percè reservation at Wallowa, congress declined to approve it.

Despite efforts by the diplomatic mission-school-educated Chief Joseph, the southern wing of the tribe was compelled, in 1877, to move from Wallowa valley to the Lapwai reservation where the two tribes of Nez Percè met once more, creating a great friction between them.

Chief Joseph wanted to avoid bloodshed but, despite his efforts some members of the Lower Nez Percè went to war and incurred the full wrath of the United States Army. General Oliver, Otis Howard and Chief Joseph had developed a mutual respect for one another but, the actions of these few people had now escalated to the point where it could not be turned around.

Chief Joseph then took command of his forces and moved them to White Bird Canyon, where on the 7th June 1877 they defeated the United States Army in the first pitched battle of what became known as the Nez Percè war. In the time that it took Howard to arrive with more men and artillery, Joseph had moved across the Clearwater River.

It was Joseph's intention to move his tribe North of the

Canadian border where the United States army would not follow him. To accomplish this however, he would have to lead them to Montana and across the Rockies and hundreds of miles of plains.

They crossed into Montana near Fort Missoula and managed to avoid or defeat the Army in a series of actions that took place across the Continental Divide and through a newly established Yellowstone National Park. As they moved across the plains, they were followed by not only Howard's troops but also by the Seventh Cavalry under a Colonel Nelson 'Bearcoat' Miles from Fort Keogh.

The Nez Percè managed to elude the Seventh Cavalry during a skirmish at Canyon Creek and crossed the Missouri at Cow Island on the 23rd September.

A week later the Nez Percè, who were also moving not only their fighting force, but their cattle and families, camped to rest in the Bear Paw Mountains. They were now finally only about a day's travel from Canada. Howard was still at least two days behind giving Joseph and his tribes time to relax.

However, meanwhile Miles had managed to get a good size cavalry within striking distance and although taking large numbers of casualties, managed to surround Joseph almost within sight of the Canadian border.

Finally with all hope gone, Joseph was forced to surrender on the 7th October 1877. He then delivered his most famous and memorable words.

'Tell General Howard that I know his heart. What he told me before, I have in my heart. I am tired of fighting. Our Chiefs are killed. Looking Glass is dead. Toohoolhoolzote is dead. It is the young men who say yes or no. He who led on the young men is dead. It is cold and we have no blankets. The children are freezing to death. I want to have time to look for my children and see how many of them I can find. Maybe I shall find them among the dead. Hear me, my chiefs! I am tired; my heart is sick and sad. From where the sun now stands I will fight no more forever'.

A small number of Nez Percè managed to cross the border and link up with Sitting Bull's Sioux but, most of them who survived were sent not to Lapwai, as promised by Miles, but back to Indian territory instead.

In 1885 what was left of the tribe returned to Lapwai but not Joseph, he was sent to Colville Reservation in Washington state, where he died on the 21st September 1904.

In 1950 the Nez Percè tribe had a population of 1400, that increased to 2251 by 1970. In 1985 the Nez Percè reservation in Idaho had a population of 2015.

These are the people who have inspired me so much in the short time that I have known them. Throughout their history they have been deservedly admired by all who knew them, both as adversaries and as friends. Their connection today with the creatures that they have shared their world with for so long, now makes them admired by a different kind of person; one who has had the privilege to know and work with these proud people.

Conflict

Many years of conflict now lay between man and wolf when, long ago, we had seen him as a creature who would willingly aid us with our hunting. We began to harness his speed, strength and devotion to family.

The wolf of today however, is seen as competition for the very food we eat. Modern society now provides us with vehicles capable of reaching great speeds over any terrain, high powered weaponry that is silent and deadly accurate over great distances and the capability of raising and growing our own food with great efficiency.

All of these qualities we once saw in the wolf, but is it so easy to forget the possibility that without the help and teaching of animals such as these, mankind may not have even survived to become the dominant species?

Every year more and more land is taken up in trying to feed our ever-increasing population. Some of these lands still play host to a few of our remaining wild predators such as bears, mountain lion and of course, wolves.

In fairness, the same modern society places just as much pressure on our farming and ranching communities as it does on our wild creatures; creatures now worlds apart, try to meet the demands of an ever expanding world. Could these two worlds ever restore the harmony and brotherhood they both once shared?

I am convinced that others who work with these animals live in constant hope that one day we can in fact restore and maintain these lost and distant memories. With our own research we always try wherever possible, (which I am sure is the intention of everyone else working with wolves) to cover every angle.

When we began our studies several years ago it was with the intention of attempting to create a more natural environment among our captive wolves, we had no idea what we would eventually discover. The avenues that this type of research has uncovered seem endless.

Whilst living with these creatures, not a day went by when I did not stop and ask myself why? Why do these animals live by sounds and voices, scent and a close-knit bond that most would think meaningless?

The answer that I came to is simply - because they have to. Their survival depends on them carrying out their daily rituals. With this thought firmly in mind we began our research.

Exploring the mind of the wolf is like looking through a window into another world. You begin to see, hear and smell some of that which their world has to offer.

Having successfully used the wolves' own forms of communication and behaviour to help strengthen, restructure, maintain and defend their home and family, we began to look at other avenues where we felt this type of research might be of help. The area that seemed to stand out above all else was that of containment; keeping the wolves in an area of our choosing, using only their own language to create the illusion that all other territories are already firmly established with their own resident packs.

We know from past history that wolves have very little respect for our fence lines, boundaries, guard dogs and even firearms. The many occasions they have been shot at possibly even wounded or having seen their pack mates killed, has not apparently dampened the hungry wolves' spirit, returning time and again for the prize that is our livestock.

But, what is it that makes our domestic animals so appealing to the wolves? The answer could be the chance of an easy meal perhaps. Every time they hunt, the wolves risk serious injury or even death. Wild herds of game have male guardians that offer some protection to the females and their young.

Many domestic herds have no use for the males. People choosing instead to use guarding or herding dogs to protect their animals. The dog is taught to guard the individuals or group of animals in their care, providing the same service as the male of that species. So what can we expect from this protection?

Reductions in the amount of herd animals killed, some domestic dog deaths and some of the wolves will be killed. Similar statistics that the wolves would face hunting in the wild, but simply facing injury or death does not stop them from hunting, they must still eat. By using guarding dogs in this way we will not stop them from hunting and killing our cattle or sheep, we will merely increase the wolves' chance of injury during their incursions.

But, is an easy meal the only reason why these animals hunt our livestock? Whilst studying breeding programmes for captive wolves we found that a pattern began to emerge over the amount and type of food that was fed to the wolves, prior to and during pregnancy.

The amount of food being fed to the breeding female over and above her usual daily quantity at these crucial times, seemed to govern the number of pups that were born.

Just as I had found with the foxes, many years prior to these

discoveries, if heavy persecution of any form takes place then the vixen seems to respond by panic breeding. She will produce a much larger litter of kits in comparison to normal.

This type of behaviour is made even more remarkable when you consider that, in most of the cases that I studied, a large majority of these young were female. Knowing that a dog fox can sire several females, the vixen may be transferring this panic onto future generations. Or, is she simply laying the foundation for the all-important balance? A balance that will need to be adjusted over the next few years, to compensate for the large number of one gender that may be born. Could this be due to the extra layers of fat that, by then, will be on their quarry, because of the temporary absence of foxes in that area?

These same factors now seem to be affecting the wolves. Could it be possible that in areas where the wolves' staple diet contains a high fat content or, that severe weather creates an increase in the number of fat cells contained within the wolves quarry, (thus creating a high fat diet) they must take other, less fatty prey in order to maintain the pack's balance to compensate for the dominance of one gender that has already been born?

This could possibly account for one other reason why wolves are seen to take sick, old or injured animals. Easy meals or are they maintaining nature's delicate balance by taking animals that will have a low fat count due to age or illness?

Unfortunately, this part of our research is still too much in the early stages for any certainty but a definite pattern has already begun to show among captive wolves. Could the same be said of their wild relatives?

The other important aspect of the wolves' food during the breeding season is the quantity of food available to the female again prior to and during pregnancy. We are currently looking into the slight increase in food at these crucial times as we feel this could dictate the amount of pups that are or are not produced.

As with all types of research, a great deal more proof needs to be obtained before we even think about offering these two findings as part of a wild wolf management programme. Only time and further studies will finally reveal the truth.

With the idea of containment still firmly in mind, we are also studying the many different scent-laying patterns in terms of changes in quantity, yearly changes, different ranks and most importantly methods of collecting the scent using different coloured trays.

During the last ten years, I have begun to see changes in the way we handle the daily welfare of our captive wolves. We continue to consider the way we achieve the delicate balance between our own interactions with the wolves in our care and allowing them to retain and express their natural behaviour.

We feel the best way to achieve this is not to enforce our rules on the wolves, but allow them to pass some of their language on to us. We believe to attempt to dominate the pack of wolves or to position ourselves as an alpha because we have the apparent right to do so, would not only be extremely dangerous, but also totally impractical. Having had an insight into the wolves' world, I know a little of what it takes to become a leader of a pack of wolves. Many of us do not possess the nature of a true alpha, our modern societies and thousands of years of domestication have removed senses that would have once placed us closer to the wolves' lifestyle. Living by smells and sounds that we can only begin to detect, our position as a leader would surely be short lived once a true contender for the alpha leadership enters or is bred into our pack.

Throughout my time with these animals, the highest rank I have held is that of beta, my current rank within the pack. I do feel that, to maintain this rank in the face of true challengers would mean having to live with the pack constantly, something I fear will not have a practical solution.

My plan for future interactions with these animals is to accept a mid-ranking position from which, we have discovered, I can move in and out of the pack without them restructuring. If I do have to leave the pack for any length of time, one of the members of the team keeps my position amongst the wolves open. Using a recording of my howl, the team will respond to the pack's calls for me, telling them that I am still close by. This type of communication seems to satisfy their natural need to replace a lost family member, ensuring that my reception, upon return, is one of welcoming curiosity and not conflict. Using this type of security over my future with the wolves may seem to some people, to be going slightly overboard, but having seen how easily and quickly they can solve simple problems with the correct incentive, I now leave absolutely nothing to chance. Maybe its the wolves' own teaching coming out in me.

Living with the wolves, I easily forget how much of their world is now running through my veins. From the special attention I get from every domestic dog that passes me, down to horses and livestock running in fear from a scent that, hundreds of years of instinct tells their brains is dangerous.

There is another side of the wolf that has been introduced to me during my time with them; that which the wolves themselves respect. Showing little or no regard for our property, the one thing that wolves respect above all else is a rival pack's territory. If wild wolf containment could help towards ending the battle between humans and our fellow predators, then this is where we feel our future research must go.

Up to now, we have only been able to use or research on captive wolves, wild wolves are slightly different in their behaviour and adjustments to our findings would have to be made. These are some of our findings so far: -

Our research has led us to three main elements of territorial defence as seen through the eyes of the wolves themselves. They are sight, sound and scent. The wolves use all of these senses to determine if it is safe to enter an area of ground that is not their own for the chance of a potential meal. Based on their findings in that area, sometimes over several days, even weeks, they will decide if they feel that it is reasonably safe for them to attempt to make a kill.

Sound: The many references throughout this book to the wolves howling to one another underlines their own need to continually communicate with rival packs. These constant territorial updates contain enough information to ensure respect for pack boundaries, whilst avoiding conflict.

Things can soon change if the wrong information is given. We can hear if the rival pack is complete. Any missing ranks among the wolves detected from their calls could result in an attempt to challenge for the right to occupy that territory. The pack needs to be large enough to hold a position in that area among the resident wolves. If numbers are too low they will be ousted. Never forget, to a wolf, more territory is more food and therefore a greater chance for pack survival.

We can hear when new-born pups make their first calls and so can easily tell if a pack has not produced pups.

The howl is an effective way to highlight pack boundaries and more importantly to maintain them but it will also provide the wolves with a great deal of information you may not want them to have.

Scent: In the wolf world scent holds the same importance and is equivalent to our vision. As with sound, so much information can be given and taken from urine, scats, scent glands and sweat. From these they can detect illness and injury, gender, rank, age, sexual development and most importantly, what the wolves have eaten is evidence that a complete or incomplete pack operates in this area.

Sight: So important to us humans, with our ability to see in great detail and a wide variety of different colours, we can almost be forgiven for allowing this most dominating of all the senses to dictate our modern world.

The Native American Indians taught us that when darkness falls and nature takes away all of her colours, this is where a different world begins; this is where we will find the wolf. Never is this more in evidence than at dusk and dawn. The pack use this time to practise hunting skills and reinforce the bonds that bind them together through scent, in readiness for the possibility of making a kill.

Night after night I have found myself in the middle of these activities. Unsure of what to do or how to communicate, the fading light itself showed me all I needed to know. Without the luxury of long range sight, the ability to detect detail and with the absence of colour vision, the wolves looked very different. I could recognise my leaders only because of their coat patterns.

In Norway, the herdsmen used to talk about the use of guarding dogs to protect their livestock against wolf attacks. Having seen these large and very protective animals, I was surprised to hear that they had not been as effective as the herdsmen had hoped. It seems the dogs had been no match for the wolves and had suffered great losses during the ongoing battles.

In early times, other countries tried to use the very fact that wolf and dog would fight. Collars with large spikes were placed around the neck of the dogs, hoping that the wolves would be either killed immediately or die at a later stage as a result of the wounds caused by them. Again this proved less than effective and more dog deaths occurred, in turn creating more bad feeling towards the wolves from the herdsmen.

We now feel that the use of guarding dogs to protect domestic livestock still remains one of our best visual deterrents, when used in conjunction with sound and scent.

As for spiked collars, wolves as young as four to five weeks old are taught the importance of avoiding sharp objects, as part of their extensive hunting training.

For many years I puzzled over the possible nutritional value in horns and antlers, because we saw them used so extensively with Zeva and Lakota, but they were not used for food, they were used in teaching. As both adults and littermates carried the antlers they would strike the young wolves, who very quickly learnt how to avoid the sharp points. Whilst it is certainly important for them to know how to bring down their quarry, it is equally important to know what to avoid. To the wolves, the large spiked collars were just another set of horns, which through daily practice were easy to avoid.

The most effective deterrent lies not in how big and defensive the guarding dog is or how big the spikes on the collar are but in the pattern on the animal's coat. Individual wolves all have their own different coat patterns, which in turn denote their rank within the pack. As the wolves reach higher positions, so their patterns change to reinforce their new rank. The same effect can be seen when wolves are ousted; their patterns will again change to signify a lower position. When you place all of these individual ranks together they will form (through scent, sound and sight) an entire pack of wolves. In order for domestic dogs to be effective in their guarding duties they must, (through these three components) make up an entire pack that is willing and able to defend its territory and whatever is in it, including domestic livestock. If the dogs do not make up a complete pack then they are no match for the wolves and their territory is up for grabs.

Using the three components, (scent, sound and sight) we have now managed to contain captive wolves in an area without the use of fencing. Even under the distraction of food being offered in this area to hungry wolves, the effects of rival packs clearly takes the highest priority among them, identifying the line that marks the boundary of the rival pack territory through sound and scent.

We tested the theory using tape recordings of rival packs and food attraction for the wolves; the resident pack's interest in the rival's presence was all too evident. The smell of the fresh kill lay only a few metres outside their own boundary, but still they did not cross over. It was as if we had placed an electric fence between the wolves and their meal, the respect these animals gave to their rivals' territory was incredible.

Day after day we tested this theory to make sure that the wolves were not merely reacting to a strange situation. For almost six months, the wolves showed no interest in crossing into their rivals' land, only in leaving their own scent just inside their own territory.

At this stage we did not use any visual deterrent because of the unnatural close proximity of the resident pack. Besides, they would be highly unlikely to meet with their neighbours in the wild and the wolves themselves place little importance on sight, preferring to use their highly developed senses of hearing and smell, in order to avoid conflict.

The tape recordings of the packs we used had all been obtained from captive wolves that we had worked with and for whom we still provided advice on their management. This allows us access to update our recordings as circumstances dictate.

Our research into containment relies heavily on the authenticity of the recordings we play to them. Because we have access to these wolves, we can also match their sound with their scent, making our rival packs as close to the real thing as possible.

The regularity with which we renew their scent, the patterns we use and the order of rank they are laid in are all important factors that need to be taken into consideration when dealing with an animal that is renowned for it's intuition.

When Zarnesti was a small pup we used to regulate his exercise; firstly because of his age, secondly because he was in with Dakota, an older wolf who could easily take him beyond his early limits and finally, due to the fact that some of his litter had been diagnosed with brittle bones. At night we secured both Zarnesti and Dakota in their house and released the pulley system that operated the door.

After only a few nights of watching this action, Dakota discovered how to raise the door by using the cable. Returning early one morning as usual we were surprised to discover that Zarnesti was out in the enclosure and very keen to run over to us, to show just what he and Dakota had achieved. However, Dakota herself was still inside the house. Having pulled on the handle of the cable she had discovered that the door would rise, letting Zarnesti out. Unfortunately, when she released it she was unable to make the gap before it slowly closed. The system itself was designed to lower slowly enough to allow an animal to escape without getting trapped underneath but still proved too quick for Dakota, as she had to get from one end of the house to the other to join her renegade companion.

Wolves are highly adept at identifying weaknesses in their prey. It follows that they can equally detect strengths and weakness in their fellow pack mates, as well as ourselves.

The importance of firstly creating, then maintaining and defending your own individual rank has already been well documented throughout this book. However, if more proof were needed, I always think back to a story I once heard about a wolf caretaker.

During the weekend, whilst off duty, he travelled down to the local bar for some well-earned liquid refreshment. Having drunk more than his fair share of alcohol he would stagger back to his accommodation by way of the wolves enclosure, having to pass close by them in order to reach his much-needed bed. As he passed the wolves, the by now large number of staff members that had gathered to watch the floor show, witnessed some unusual behaviour from them!

As if driven by instinct, the animals seemed to be displaying what looked like prey drive. The next morning everyone who had witnessed this behaviour had finally satisfied themselves that it must have been the smell of the alcohol that had provoked the strange reaction in the wolves.

Some domestic dogs reacting badly to the smell of alcohol but usually only if the animal had suffered a bad experience as a direct result of the smell, making a connection with the two components. These wolves had no cause to even identify with this smell, let alone react to it.

Further investigation uncovered an old video recording of a wild wolf kill made on a bison calf with an injured leg. Exploring all avenues, a tape was then made of the gentleman returning from the bar on his next weekend off. Once the two tapes were played together, the truth behind the wolves' behaviour became apparent. The injured calf and the intoxicated man's movement almost mirrored one another. Tests were then made to try and confirm their theories, resulting in clear evidence that it was in fact the man's movements, not the smell of the drink, that had caused the wolves to react, sadly leaving his future with that pack hanging in the balance.

We still believe and maintain that the safest way to interact with the wolves is through family bonds. Many people who work with wolves throughout the world will have their own methods of interaction and may totally disagree with these studies. But having personally created, defended and maintained my own position among these animals and observed the positive results I have gained, I firmly stand by my decision to live with these wolves over many years throughout their daily lives, sharing their ups and downs, their highs and their lows. The experiences I have gained will remain with the team and myself forever.

Gaining a sample of urine from any wild animal can be a tricky affair, sometimes next to impossible. In order for our studies to work we would need a good supply of the animals' scent working through every rank. The collection of urine is achieved by placing different coloured and scented trays in the wolves' enclosure at set points around their territorial boundaries. The trays seem to attract the wolves, who seem almost compelled to scent over them, giving us the samples we require whilst reducing greatly the amount of stress on the animal itself.

Scats are collected using bags to pick them up and then tying them off. Because of the wolves' rank structure and the type of feeding our wolves receive, it is easy to identify each individual by its own scat. Largely determined by the quality and quantity, the alpha's droppings are completely different to those of a lower ranking wolf and then subsequently a change in these two types of the scat's components will occur as the rank structure feeds in order of status.

Colour, texture, smell and quantity are just some of the factors that we can gain information from just by looking. Imagine what another wolf would determine from the scats.

The cycle that the wolves are currently feeding on, the type of food they are eating and the quantity that they are consuming all reveal the wolf's story and its immediate past history.

We are also currently looking into the correct use of guarding dogs as a visual deterrent for wild wolves. Having seen a good deal of different types of these animals, we feel that our final choice would have to posses some or all of the following criteria:

An ability and natural instinct to avoid conflict as opposed to the high defensive drive that has been used in the past.

The animal must also have the correct coat pattern, underlining the rank that it holds with-in the pack, with each of the remaining family members all being similarly denoted in rank by their own pattern variation. This will give the wolves the best chance to gain the information they require without a fight.

Training of these animals must we feel, mirror the teaching of the young wolf pups, covering the many aspects of communication, behaviour, rank structure and most importantly the survival skills that young wolves would need to keep them safe.

Finally the guarding dogs role will be to defend their own territory, not the herd that dwells within it. If the dogs will defend in this way then not only do they protect their territory preventing any trespassers from entering; they will also offer protection to whatever may be living in it.

Due to the nature of the training these animals would receive, it is important to point out that this type of training would not make them an acceptable choice in our own homes or modern society. These types of animals provide a working function - they are not pets. Teaching them the strict social structure unique to the wolves means that their rank system would be identical to that of the wolves, making them very overpowering around small children and juveniles.

The importance and success of this type of research relies heavily on a number of factors. Authenticity and the need for a complete pack rank structure are just two of these aspects. Complete packs not only communicate with rival families; they also provide information to the lone wolves who live in the buffer zones close by. If one of the ranks in our pack is missing they will know this and begin attempting to occupy the vacant position, which again could cause problems on our farms and ranches.

Imitating a pack of wolves is a very demanding and time consuming task; we speak from experience! But the positive impact that this type of enrichment provides to our wolves, far outweighs the dedication needed to carry it out.

The animals we have worked with have given us so much. We hope the knowledge we have gained will offer us a chance to give them something in return.

18

What the future holds

Like most people who have ever worked with animals, I am very reluctant to look to what the future might offer for fear that, what lies there may not be what we want to see.

More and more of our natural wilderness disappears each year, making our plight to secure a future for the creatures that live there harder and harder. We all live in the hope that one day mankind will come to realise the importance of these lands and of the many mammals, birds, fish, reptiles and insects that live there.

For a number of years now, we have rented an area of land from where we could conduct our research. Heavily wooded with natural undergrowth, it provides us with a natural environment to carry out our studies. Home to our two wolves, Zarnesti and Dakota, it is the place where we have been able to learn, educate others and research our future plans.

Now we feel it is time for ourselves and our wolves to move on. With our captive management programmes and wolf containment planning, we have also identified another area of captive wolf research that we feel needs to be explored - that of bloodlines.

Within the United Kingdom, studies of wolves in captivity have underlined the need for new bloodlines to strengthen existing packs, in an attempt to reduce the amount of inbreeding that may cause future problems among our wolves.

Although there is little concrete evidence to state that

inbreeding among wolves currently proves a problem to them, we have looked at some of the possible effects that a weakened bloodline may have on the wolf and compared them with existing data on our domestic dogs. We found some of the results of canine inbreeding to be similarly evident among some of our captive packs.

In the wild, the life expectancy of a wolf is only between six and seven years. A male or female may make alpha status at the age of around three years, giving them on average three to four years to pass on their genes as leaders. This is not a great deal of time when you come to compare the statistics concerning captive wolves. The same age of reaching leadership status can occur in captive wolves as with wild, two to three years. However, the captive wolves do not have to contend with the large quantity of predators that their wild brothers face and they are not subject to parasites or the prospect of starvation. This makes their life expectancy jump massively to sixteen or seventeen years of age. Fed on the best quality food, the alpha pairing are often more than capable of breeding right up until their deaths.

Although the female wolf (unlike some of our domestic dogs who have two seasons a year) only comes into season once a year, between her and the alpha male they could produce thirteen to fourteen generations of the same bloodline, completely saturating that pack with their genes.

With the research that we have undertaken, we now feel that new bloodlines could be introduced to captive packs using their own natural method of communication, thereby cutting down on the amount of inbreeding.

The infiltration would be based on the wolves' own method of natural dispersal. Wolves who have been ousted from one pack would naturally look either to join another pack or to begin their own. Using the methods described earlier, we feel we could now introduce these new bloodlines into existing packs without too much disturbance to both parties, one of the many benefits of working on the wolves' natural instincts.

Having asked ourselves the all important questions of whether this could be done and then more importantly should it be done, taking into consideration all the implications for the wolves themselves, our trials have shown that, so far, the benefits to the wolves are considerably high. Because we are dealing with an area that is perfectly natural to them, there have been no negative effects, apart from sleep deprivation on the part of the team!

Now that the studies have been confirmed through their infancy, it is time for us to seek a greater understanding of these areas so that if or when they should ever be needed, then we will be prepared to deal with them.

We are looking at the possibility of opening a wolf sanctuary with a research and educational centre. Set in the wolves' natural surroundings, the centre will provide a large untouched area of woodland for them to occupy. This will provide keepers and staff, as well as students of all aspects of animal behaviour, a chance to see and learn from these creatures firsthand whilst carrying out the all important areas of research that are so badly needed for the future of the wolf.

The centre would also provide a sanctuary for the accidental breeding of pups who cannot, for whatever reason, be homed at their place of birth, with a view to re-homing these animals, after training, into a pack environment. This would be under the strict understanding that the establishment then undergoes a full pack management programme to prevent any future unwanted breeding.

The aim of the proposed programme is to reduce the number of unwanted wolf pups born into captivity causing overcrowding and behavioural problems that can lead to injury and possible deaths.

The second aspect of the sanctuary provides a number of functions concerning wolf protection, training and bloodlines, both for wild and captive animals. During wild wolf release there are nearly always animals that stray from the containment area, usually due to the fact that our farms and ranches have now moved to within a few miles of the national parks or as a result of natural dispersal. Having strayed onto neighbouring farming lands, the wolves have become a problem and concern, not only for the farmers but also the release teams and biologists who have to find a solution to this problem.

Some other countries view wolves in a completely different way - as pests that attack and kill their livestock. They are dealt with accordingly, usually resulting in their death. People cannot be blamed (in most cases) for wanting to protect their livelihoods from the wolves. In many cases they have simply not been given the education that we have on the lifestyles, behaviour and needs of these animals.

Not understanding an animal can lead to fear and false accusations, the guilty parties who you fear have just killed and eaten your only supply of fresh milk that was to feed your family for that entire year.

Recovering wolves into these areas would serve only to destroy the animal that is to be released, along with the already depleted numbers of wolves who live there. Without educating the people who have to live beside the wolf, we may be signing the death warrants of these animals by releasing them and indeed, we may be facing their departure altogether from that area, if we do not act quickly.

The Sanctuary would not only provide a home for any wolves facing such action. The animals themselves could produce the future packs for that area with the correct breeding programme.

Initially the removal of these animals from the wild and placement of them in a captive environment can be very distressing for them and should only be attempted as a final option to save the wolf.

Park rules or financial needs would not govern the sanctuary. We rely on education and research, so the amount of human contact with these animals, to begin with, will be kept to the absolute minimum.

Because our aim is to maintain the wolves in our care in conditions as close to nature as possible, for any animal that is recovered to the centre from the wild, the adjustment to this captive lifestyle will not be too great.

There is one more important factor that we have researched into. Many of these problem wolves will be the result of natural dispersal and as such will be looking for their own territory in which to begin their own packs.

But what of these wolves once they arrive at their new safe haven? Well, careful studies will be made into the area from which the wolves came if one is not already in place. Then members of the team will travel to these areas to provide help with an education and a management programme, for as long as deemed necessary, to ensure the safe return to the wild of these wolves.

The aim of the programme is to maintain a strong and healthy bloodline by introducing the wild strains from the same subspecies of wolf but from different areas. We will be able to strengthen their existing bloodlines, so that if and when the people of that area are ready, through education, to accept the wolves back, stronger offspring of the original wolves can then be bred and prepared for wild release.

The arrival of these wolves will also aid us in our work throughout the UK, providing newer and stronger bloodlines to captive packs, helping to reduce the amount of inbreeding and possible resultant decline in health among captive wolves.

The main aim with these animals is to always have a breeding programme ready to produce strong and healthy offspring should, heaven forbid, there ever be a need to restock wild populations of wolves once more.

As for wild wolves, with each passing day more of their natural habitat is eaten up by our towns and cities' rapid growth. The wide dispersal rate of the wolf, that once kept their bloodlines strong and free

from disease, is slowly diminishing. If not immediately, then in the near future our wild wolves will possibly need the very same help that we now offer to our captive animals, making this type of research into bloodlines invaluable.

If the wolves have taught me one thing in my time amongst them, it is to always plan for tomorrow. This is a view shared by my Indian teachers. Taken together and coming from the two sets of families, whose teachings and wisdom I now live my own family life by; I welcome this guidance towards the answers I will need for the future.

For Wolf Pack Management and our new centre, we face the future with renewed optimism. The wolves' popularity has steadily increased thanks to the many people who have given their dedication and time in promoting these animals in their true light. We shall continue with our studies for as long as it takes, to get the answers needed to give the wolf a fighting chance in our modern and every expanding society.

CHAPTER 19

A new beginning

As the sun once more rises on a new day, I again alight from my now familiar resting-place beneath the cover of the branches of the old hollow tree overlooking the wolves. Zeva's pups have now grown and are almost mature in appearance but, have still maintained their juvenile status among the pack.

Zeva herself has just begun her season, slightly earlier than normal, in fact almost one whole month, yet another sign that our seasons are fast changing and with it our wildlife and plants' life cycles.

In the clearing, surrounded by the cover of the huge trees, the young wolves play with their mother and two or three other adults. They are preparing themselves for the next generation of pups that will arrive somewhere between sixty and sixty three days after Zeva conceives. The three pups from last year will play a vital role in the unborn offspring's' future, having themselves just come through the first few months of life among the adults, they offer one of the most informative parts of the young wolves' education.

Over the first six months of their lives, these juveniles will help to teach their younger brothers and sisters through a gentle and careful balance of play and education under the watchful eye of the pups' parents and nannies.

As yet, the alpha and the remaining adult males seem to show little or no interest in Zeva's season. However, this lack of interest hides a very clever introduction by Zeva herself into her changing condition by

scent. She moves around the adult males with her tail raised just enough to alert them to the new odour that she now emits. Over the next three to four weeks this scent will change, informing her chosen mate that she is receptive and ready to breed.

Not only is her own odour used in this instinctive advertisement, she also lays a unique scent pattern on the ground in and around the packs' territorial pathways, ensuring that her time of copulation is not missed by the males that frequently visit these boundaries.

During this time she will not remain loyal to the alpha male. To ensure that the future wolves for the pack are produced during her receptive time, she will mate with any one of the adult males if the opportunity arises. It is up to the alpha male at this time to ensure that there are no other candidates for the position of fathering her pups. Yet again we can see the importance of a correct rank structure among the wolves. If the alpha leadership is not firmly in place, this time of very high tension among the wolves could result in large numbers of serious injuries among both sexes, under the distraction of breeding. Both alphas need all of their leadership qualities during these times, from within the wolf packs' social structure and beyond, because most of their respect is earned from their ability to defend the pack and its territory. That can only be achieved by giving them something to defend against, rival wolves.

Throughout the natural world, thoughts now seem to lay firmly with producing young; the two owls constantly refresh their monogamous bond under the cover of darkness, whilst at the same time warding off any would be challenges to their territory.

Off to my right, the large herd of deer has begun their rutting season among the males, the young desperate to triumph over old bucks so that they too may sire the next calves. Nature's reproduction is truly one of the greatest wonders.

Seeing the careful balance being maintained to give all of her creatures and plants an equal chance of survival makes me realise just how much thought and work we need to apply if we are to help animals in our care. Studying not only the way in which that mammal, bird, reptile or plant's own world revolves but, also how it fits into the overall plan and takes its rightful place within nature's intricate ecosystem.

Returning to the south from Wiltshire, it is evident that every wolf pack is the same in experiencing premature seasons this year. Our colleagues from Paradise Wildlife Park have confirmed that their own female has already been through her own season and finished, making her roughly two weeks earlier than the rest of the wolves in our care. Having confirmed that Sheba, the old female is not as yet in season, we then check on our own wolf, Dakota. She has shown both behavioural and vocal signs for a number of days, so it is time to check whether she has a visible showing.

As the two wolves in our care are used in an ambassadorial role for their species, they are used to being examined but even so, we always make sure that we approach the wolves as they would expect to be approached by a higher or lower ranking animal. This is done so as not to confuse the wolf and cause him or her unnecessary stress.

I move towards Dakota with my body tall and confident, telling her that she is about to be approached by a higher ranking animal, my head slightly turned to one side, face smooth, teeth covered and my eyes soft, almost closed. I meet her gaze for only a split second, telling her of my intentions. She responds, letting me know that she is comfortable by licking her nose just below the nostrils, something I have seen from her many times, whilst I am moving towards her.

Following a mutual exchange of facial expressions, our eyes soft, almost closed, we have now exchanged enough communication to symbolise our intent. All that now remains for me to do is to move slightly to one side of her, arcing my approach, to inform her that she does not have to move as her leader approaches. If I had wished for her to adjust her position to allow me to pass then I would have moved directly towards her in a straight line, making my intentions clear long before I passed her.

This simple exchange of mutual language has now brought me safely and without confusion to Dakota's side. As I move in above her, to again emphasise my higher rank, she adopts a position of trust, offering her underside up to me, perfectly safe in her respect for one of her leaders.

Gently, I use the outside of my fingers to begin the all-important pack grooming. Using a comb or a brush on a wild animal such as the wolf is, in my opinion, pointless. The same pack bond, cleaning and welfare check can just as easily be carried out by using the method I have adopted. The significant difference is that it is more natural to the animal this way, whilst at the same time reinforcing valuable scent ties.

Having checked Dakota and confirmed that she is indeed in season, it is decided that we will also carry out a routine health check on

Zarnesti, the young male. Zarnesti has always taken confidence from having Dakota close by him, so whenever we examine him we always give him the security of his leader right by his side.

Using a bolder wolf to install confidence in a lower ranking animal is something we use all the time. The difference it makes in relieving tension is incredible and the character expansion in this young animal, under Dakota's guidance, is clear for all to see. Building Zarnesti's trust in the people who handle him is extremely important, both for the young wolf and the people who care for him.

Zarnesti's youth should not cause a problem with breeding. The fact that he is a European wolf, whereas Dakota is an American timber wolf, means we would never breed from the two different subspecies. Also, the possible health problems that were identified among his littermates make him much too high-risk to consider breeding from him even among his own kind.

Knowing the strange things that can and have happened when dealing with Mother Nature, nothing can be left to chance, so Dakota's season will be naturally suppressed by a higher ranking animal. This will show her that the time has not yet come for her to pass on her genes to future generations. This task will fall to Jan. As high ranking female, it is

her right to suppress lower ranking animals, including Dakota. She merely uses the same language that would have been taught to Dakota as a pup to reinforce her dominant position.

Among the wolves, suppression is not achieved by increasing the intensity of communication. Despite the beliefs of many humans, it is achieved by using the same balance of discipline and language, only the frequency of usage increases. This applies a natural contraceptive among the wolves that ensures only the high ranking animals produce pups. No drugs are needed, that could cause detrimental long-term effects. Using this method ensures that when Dakota's time comes for her to pass on her genes she will do so as alpha of her own pack and she will have earned the right to breed under the rules of the wolves themselves.

The importance of breeding and viable bloodlines among the wolves and all other animals has been told for thousands of years. The many different stories that I have heard from people of diverse origins only serve to underline this importance. One such story I heard told by some visitors whilst out in Canada…

Long ago, the old ones had all gathered together, to watch the strange behaviour of their fellow beings. Master of all Breath was also watching, he saw some jumping among the trees and running about.

Confused by what they saw, the old ones asked Master of all Breath what these strange beings were.

Master of all Breath replied, 'What do you see old ones?'

'They are like panthers.' replied one of the old ones.

'Then from this day forth they shall be called Panthers'.

Other beings then began leaping and jumping.

'What of these beings?' asked another old one.

'They look like deer.'

Master of all Breath spoke again; 'Then from this day forth they shall travel as deer.'

Looking towards the treetops a voice was heard asking, 'What of the beings that are hopping among the tall branches and leaves of the trees? They are like the birds.'

Master of all Breath spoke again; 'From this day forth they shall be known as birds.'

Some of the beings were very fat and made a great noise as they walked. 'They are like bears,' said one of the old ones.

'Then from this day forth they shall live as bears,' said Master of all Breath.

After a time many of the creatures began to leave. When they returned each one of them had changed. The old ones once more spoke to Master of all Breath.

'Some now have black stripes near their eyes, they look like racoons.'

'Then that kind shall be Racoons,' said Master of all Breath.

Some beings then entered the water. 'They shall be known as beaver and mink,' said Master of all Breath.

Soon other beings began to take other forms that could bend the saplings or burrow into the ground.

'These shall be known as wind and potato,' said Master of all Breath and so each thing was born.

After giving everything a form on the earth, Master of all Breath then spoke to them all. He told them never to marry their own kind, but to marry those from other clans. All of the red people know their own clans that they belong to. They do not marry in their own clans; if they did they would never increase.

Watching Jan interacting with Dakota I begin to realise just what the last seven years of living with these wolves has been all about. The close bonds that both myself and the rest of the team have forged with these animals will remain with us for our entire lives.

They have become my second family. With them I have shared secrets untold to anyone before, fed, slept and breathed the very same air and in return they have given me the greatest gift of all; their own language.

They have welcomed not an animal into their world but a man crossing the many boundaries that have separated our worlds for so long. I have seen beyond their bloodthirsty image, to a gentle togetherness that even overshadows our own.

If the Great Spirit gave me this time again and said change what you will, my time with my wolf brothers would remain exactly the same. I have lost so many of our brothers and sisters since I first joined with them and yet every day their memories live on in my thoughts through the many teachings they have given me.

Now, looking to the future, it is my chance to pass on everything that has ever been taught to me by the wolves.

Dakota's time to breed has not yet come. She is a fine beta and someday she will make an even better alpha, with all the balance and trust that I have come to expect from her. The games we played in the tall grass when first she and Zarnesti arrived, to build the bonds that have now served to make the three of us a family, now seem so long ago.

Shortly, with the arrival of a new bloodline, my reign as Dakota's leader will come to an end. I must rightly make way to allow a new alpha to pair bond with her and create the future not only of wolves within the UK, but wherever there is a need to strengthen their bloodlines or numbers.

She and her new mate must create the type of friendship that she and I had once shared. Like a father who has just given his daughter's hand to her future partner, I am filled with just a little apprehension at entrusting her safety to someone other than me.

Zarnesti and I have a different bond to that which I share with Dakota. He will remain the one wolf who I will always watch over. I have always likened the wolves' pack to that of our own families. With this in mind,

Zarnesti would almost certainly be my younger brother, for most of the time he is happy to deal with his new found adulthood, only to display all the vulnerability of one so young when someone or something causes him to hurry to my side for protection.

These last few comments as I bring this book to a close may seem a little sad; they are intended to be far from sadness. I now look to a future that will bring me even closer to my wolf family. As one of the future pups' guardians, it will be my responsibility to pass on all that I have learnt to them, keeping alive the wolves ancestry.

Somewhere it is written that there is a place where the answers to all the questions we have ever asked can be found. I believe that such a place lies deep inside each and every one of us.

Like the wolves themselves, our short time in this world gives us some of these answers and these answers we must pass on to our children. One of the questions to be answered is, how can we once more live in complete harmony with our fellow creatures and maintain natures' delicate balance?

Here is where I would like to turn to one of the greatest minds in our history, Albert Einstein. It has apparently become clear that our technology has far outweighed our humanity. Einstein devoted his entire life to creating some of the technology scientists still use today. Einstein, among others of his own profession, still gave himself the luxury of looking beyond science and technology, firmly believing in such things as reincarnation. Was it his hunger to seek these answers that allowed him to see beyond science? Or, was it that, whilst seeking these answers, he too found areas that science and technology alone cannot explain.

Once, whilst out studying wild wolves, a group of scientists led by two native American biologists from that area, saw three figures moving down from the far ridge line to the valley below. The wolves were dark in colour and very large in size compared to the animals that lived there. Puzzled by what they saw before them, they decided to watch the wolves'

movements and witness what they would do next. To the astonishment of them all, the three animals that no-one had ever seen in that area before, found, attacked and killed a bear. The bear was not eaten neither was it cached or taken to hungry pups waiting near by. The bear was simply left lying by the tree where it had fallen. The three male wolves, as they had now been identified by use of powerful telescopes, left as quickly and quietly as they had arrived.

Curious as to the nature of this seemingly motiveless attack, the men left their observation post and travelled down to where the bear's body lay. When they arrived at the scene even more of this mystery began to unfold. The bear that had been killed was the same animal that had been causing problems in the nearby villages. No one as yet had been injured but the animal had done a large amount of damage and it had been felt that it was only a matter of time before someone was hurt.

Men from the village and local authorities had searched for the bear but, were unable to find it before the animal injured a small child whilst out with his dog.

The scientist began to search for answers as to the wolves' reasons for travelling into this area. Food? But they had not eaten. Territory? But they had not stayed. A mate? Maybe.

The two Native American biologists simply thanked their ancestors who, having taken the form of these wolves, had entered their world to help them to stop the bear.

Our differences are clear; because our minds tell us that it is not possible to believe in something we think does not exist, we try even harder to dispel that which is often the truth.

However, sometimes these insights can come from an inner strength that not even the body carrying them knows of. Only the great spirit creatures that visit these individuals from time to time, giving them the honour of their form, know that their secrets are still safe with them and must not yet be told to those who do not understand.

One day the many messengers who still carry their stories may all once more tell us of these creatures.

As for the future of the remaining wolves in our care, time will tell their own stories. Fang's fall from leadership. Maggie's rise through the pack's hierarchy to maybe challenge her own mother for the right to lead their pack. Not forgetting little Mo, the wolf we all thought would be destined for a life at the bottom of the pack. Last but by no means least, Zac and his new mate.

Could it be that after so long without producing pups, finally, in a few short months we will once again be watching over another generation of wolves? To once more face a new beginning...

More Publications from Rainbow

Happy Dogs Happy Winners (Revised Edition Published 2003)
Complete manual of obedience training. Endorsed by top obedience
champion handlers, this book is ideal for complete beginners and more
experienced handlers alike. Each exercise is covered with a step by step
approach to enable the discerning trainer to work their way from the
beginner class right through to championship level competition.
First published 1993 Rainbow Publishing. Second revised edition 2003,
Rainbow Publishing. ISBN 1-899057-00-5
Price £12.95 Plus £1.50 P&P UK, (£2.90 P&P rest of the world).
First edition available in German Translation Price £14.95 Plus P&P as above.

Dog Training Instructor's Manual
This much acclaimed instructor's 'bible', is a comprehensive book which
includes all you need to know to teach others the art of dog training. From
setting up a school, organising classes and courses, how to keep the pupils
attention and how to conduct yourself. It includes advice on puppy
groups, problem dogs, specialist training as well as standard pet dog
control.
Published 2000, Rainbow Publishing. ISBN 1-899057-02-1
Price £12.95 Plus £2.00 P&P UK (£2.90 rest of the world)

Booklets Available Direct From Rainbow Publishing

Clicker and Target Training - Teaching for Fun and Competition
Second Edition
Author Angela White. Published by Rainbow, 2003. £4.99 Plus 50p P&P UK
(£1.00 P&P Europe, £1.50 P&P rest of the world)
Order 10 or more copies 10% discount
Other Booklets by Angela White...

How to be top dog

How to recognise, deal with and treat dominant dogs in a domestic
environment. From puppy growls, to viscous attacks, this booklet helps
owners to avoid confrontations and get the behaviour under their own
control.

Home Alone Canine

Getting dogs used to being alone, how to combat stress. Dealing with the
problems owners and their dogs face when they are left alone. Including
chewing, barking, urinating, defecating as well as associated behaviours.

Dog Training

Basic techniques for getting control of your pet. All based on kind,
motivational methods of training that work with the dog's own desires.
Includes: sit, down, stand, come back, walk on a loose lead, leave and don't
jump up.

Above 3 booklets published by Rainbow, 2003. £3.99 inc. P&P UK (£1.00
P&P Europe, £1.50 P&P rest of the world)
Order 10 or more copies 10% discount